CAMBRIDGE LIBRARY COLLECTION

Books of enduring scholarly value

Women's Writing

The later twentieth century saw a huge wave of academic interest in women's writing, which led to the rediscovery of neglected works from a wide range of genres, periods and languages. Many books that were immensely popular and influential in their own day are now studied again, both for their own sake and for what they reveal about the social, political and cultural conditions of their time. A pioneering resource in this area is Orlando: Women's Writing in the British Isles from the Beginnings to the Present (http://orlando.cambridge.org), which provides entries on authors' lives and writing careers, contextual material, timelines, sets of internal links, and bibliographies. Its editors have made a major contribution to the selection of the works reissued in this series within the Cambridge Library Collection, which focuses on non-fiction publications by women on a wide range of subjects from astronomy to biography, music to political economy, and education to prison reform.

A Letter to the Queen on Lord Chancellor Cranworth's Marriage and Divorce Bill

Caroline Norton (1808–77) was a Victorian author and campaigner for social reform, especially reform of women's legal rights. In this lucidly written account Norton describes how, upon marriage, women became legally 'non-existent': they could not bring cases to court; they could not enter into a contract; they could not instigate a divorce and their possessions, earnings and any bequests made to them automatically became their husband's property. Norton explains how this lack of legal autonomy affected women if they became estranged from their husbands, using her own experiences for illustration and recommending changes which would improve women's legal position. Published in 1855 when Parliament was debating the subject of divorce reform, this volume shows the legal position of women at this time. It provides the opinions of contemporary legislators in support and opposition on the issues of women's legal rights and reform of divorce laws. For more information on this author, see http://orlando.cambridge.org/public/svPeople?person_id=nortca

Cambridge University Press has long been a pioneer in the reissuing of out-of-print titles from its own backlist, producing digital reprints of books that are still sought after by scholars and students but could not be reprinted economically using traditional technology. The Cambridge Library Collection extends this activity to a wider range of books which are still of importance to researchers and professionals, either for the source material they contain, or as landmarks in the history of their academic discipline.

Drawing from the world-renowned collections in the Cambridge University Library, and guided by the advice of experts in each subject area, Cambridge University Press is using state-of-the-art scanning machines in its own Printing House to capture the content of each book selected for inclusion. The files are processed to give a consistently clear, crisp image, and the books finished to the high quality standard for which the Press is recognised around the world. The latest print-on-demand technology ensures that the books will remain available indefinitely, and that orders for single or multiple copies can quickly be supplied.

The Cambridge Library Collection will bring back to life books of enduring scholarly value (including out-of-copyright works originally issued by other publishers) across a wide range of disciplines in the humanities and social sciences and in science and technology.

A Letter to the Queen
on Lord Chancellor
Cranworth's Marriage
and Divorce Bill

CAROLINE SHERIDAN NORTON

CAMBRIDGE
UNIVERSITY PRESS

CAMBRIDGE UNIVERSITY PRESS

Cambridge, New York, Melbourne, Madrid, Cape Town, Singapore,
São Paolo, Delhi, Dubai, Tokyo

Published in the United States of America by Cambridge University Press, New York

www.cambridge.org
Information on this title: www.cambridge.org/9781108018364

© in this compilation Cambridge University Press 2010

This edition first published 1855
This digitally printed version 2010

ISBN 978-1-108-01836-4 Paperback

This book reproduces the text of the original edition. The content and language reflect
the beliefs, practices and terminology of their time, and have not been updated.

Cambridge University Press wishes to make clear that the book, unless originally published
by Cambridge, is not being republished by, in association or collaboration with, or
with the endorsement or approval of, the original publisher or its successors in title.

A LETTER TO THE QUEEN

ON

LORD CHANCELLOR CRANWORTH'S

MARRIAGE AND DIVORCE BILL.

BY

THE HON. MRS. NORTON.

"𝔒nlɒ a 𝔴oman's ḥair."

<small>THACKERAY'S LECTURE ON SWIFT.</small>

LONDON:

LONGMAN, BROWN, GREEN AND LONGMANS.

1855.

A LETTER TO THE QUEEN.

MADAM,

On Tuesday, June 13th, of last session, Lord Chancellor Cranworth brought forward a measure for the reform of the Marriage laws of England; which measure was afterwards withdrawn. In March, 1855, in this present session, the Solicitor General stated, that a bill on the same subject was "nearly prepared," and would be brought forward "immediately after the Easter recess." On May 10th, being pressed to name a time, he stated that it would be proposed "*as soon as the House had expressed an opinion on the Testamentary Jurisdiction Bill.*" That time has not arrived: and meanwhile,—as one who has grievously suffered, and is still suffering, under the present imperfect state of the law,— I address your Majesty on the subject.

I do not do so in the way of appeal. The vague romance of "carrying my wrongs to the foot of the throne," forms no part of my intention: for I know the throne is powerless to redress them. I know those pleasant tales of an earlier and simpler time, when oppressed subjects travelled to the presence of some glorious prince or princess, who instantly set their affairs to rights without reference to law, are quaint old histories, or fairy fables, fit only for the amusement of children.

I connect your Majesty's name with these pages from a different motive; for two reasons: of which one, indeed, is a sequence to the other. First, because I desire to point out the grotesque anomaly which ordains that married women shall be "non-existent" in a country governed by a female Sovereign; and secondly, because, whatever measure for the reform of these statutes may be proposed, it cannot become "the law of the land" without your Majesty's assent and sign manual. In England there is no Salique law. If there were,—if the principles which guide all legislation for the inferior sex in this country, were carried out in their integrity as far as the throne,—your Majesty would be by birth a subject, and Hanover and England would be still under one King.

It is not so. Your Majesty is Queen of England; Head of the Church; Head of the Law; Ruler of millions of men; and the assembled Senate who meet to debate and frame legislative enactments in each succeeding year, *begin* their sessional labours by reverently listening to that clear woman's voice, — rebellion against whose command is treason.

In the year 1845, on the occasion of the opening of the new Hall of Lincoln's Inn, your Majesty honoured that Hall with your presence: when His Royal Highness Prince Albert was invited to become a Barrister: "the keeping of " his terms and exercises, and the payment of " all fees and expenses, being dispensed with." It was an occasion of great pomp and rejoicing. No reigning sovereign had visited the Inns of Court since Charles II., in 1671. In the magnificent library of Lincoln's Inn, seated on a chair of state (Prince Albert standing), your Majesty held a levee; and received an address from the benchers, barristers, and students-at-law, which was read by the treasurer on his knee: thanking your Majesty for the proof given by your presence of your "gracious regard for the profession of the law,"—offering congratulations "on the great amendments of the law,

" effected since your Majesty's accession;" and affirming that "the pure glory of those labours must be dear to your Majesty's heart."

To that address your Majesty was graciously pleased to return a suitable answer; adding,—
"I gladly testify my respect for the profession
" of the law; by which I am aided in administer-
"ing JUSTICE, and in maintaining the preroga-
"tive of the Crown and the rights of my peo-
"ple."

A banquet followed. The health of the new barrister, the Prince Consort, was drunk with loud cheers. His Royal Highness put on a student's gown, over his Field Marshal's uniform, and so wore it on returning from the Hall; and then that glittering courtly vision—of a young beloved queen, with ladies in waiting, and attendant officers of state, and dignitaries in rich dresses, melted out of the solemn library; and left the dingy law courts once more to the dull quiet, which had been undisturbed by such a gorgeous sight for nearly two hundred years. Only, on the grand day of the following Trinity term, the new Barrister, His Royal Highness Prince Albert, dined in the Hall as a Bencher, in compliment to those who had elected him.

Now this was not a great mockery; but a

great ceremony. It was entered into with the serious loyalty of faithful subjects: with the enthusiasm of attached hearts: and I know not what sight could be more graceful or touching, than the homage of those venerable and learned men to their young female sovereign. The image of Lawful Power, coming in such fragile person, to meet them on that vantage ground of Justice, where students are taught, by sublime theories, how Right can be defended against Might, the poor against the rich, the weak against the strong, in their legal practice; and how entirely the civilised intelligence of the nineteenth century rejects, as barbarous, those bandit rules of old, based on the " simple plan,"

> " That they should take, who have the power,
> And they should keep, who *can*."

It was the very poetry of allegiance, when the Lord Chancellor and the other great law officers did obeisance in that Hall to their Queen; and the Treasurer knelt at a woman's feet, to read of the amendments in that great stern science by which governments themselves are governed; whose thrall all nations submit to; whose value even the savage acknowledges,—and checks by its means the wild liberty he enjoys, with some rude form of polity and order.

Madam,—I will not do your Majesty the injustice of supposing, that the very different aspect the law wears in England for the female sovereign and the female subject, must render you indifferent to what those subjects may suffer; or what reform may be proposed, in the rules more immediately affecting them. I therefore submit a brief and familiar exposition of the laws relating to women,—as taught and practised in those Inns of Court, where your Majesty received homage, and Prince Albert was elected a Bencher.

———

A married woman in England has *no legal existence:* her being is absorbed in that of her husband. Years of separation or desertion cannot alter this position. Unless divorced by special enactment in the House of Lords, the legal fiction holds her to be "*one*" with her husband, even though she may never see or hear of him.

She has no possessions, unless by special settlement; her property is *his* property. Lord Ellenborough mentions a case in which a sailor bequeathed "all he was worth" to a woman he cohabited with; and afterwards married, in the West Indies, a woman of considerable fortune. At this man's death it was held,—notwithstanding the hardship of the case,—that the will swept away from his widow, in favour of his mistress, every shilling of the property. It is now provided that a will shall be revoked by marriage: but the claim of *the husband* to all that is his wife's exists in full force. An English wife has no legal right even to her clothes or ornaments; her husband may take them and sell them if he pleases, even though they be the gifts of relatives or friends, or bought before marriage.

An English wife cannot make a will. She may have children or kindred whom she may earnestly desire to benefit;—she may be separated from her husband, who may be living with a mistress; no matter: the law gives what she has to him, and no will she could make would be valid.

An English wife cannot legally claim her own earnings. Whether wages for manual labour, or payment for intellectual exertion, whether she weed potatoes, or keep a school, her salary is *the husband's*; and he could compel a second payment, and treat the first as void, if paid to the wife without his sanction.

An English wife may not leave her husband's

house. Not only can he sue her for " restitution
of conjugal rights," but he has a right to enter the
house of any friend or relation with whom she
may take refuge, and who may " harbour her,"
—as it is termed,—and carry her away by force,
with or without the aid of the police.

If the wife sue for separation for cruelty, it
must be " cruelty that endangers life or limb,"
and if she has once forgiven, or, in legal phrase,
" *condoned*" his offences, she cannot plead them;
though her past forgiveness only proves that she
endured as long as endurance was possible.

If her husband take proceedings for a divorce,
she is not, in the first instance, allowed to defend
herself. She has no means of proving the falsehood of his allegations. She is not represented
by attorney, nor permitted to be considered a
party to the suit between him and her supposed
lover, for " damages." Lord Brougham affirmed
in the House of Lords: " *in that action the cha-*
" *racter of the woman was at immediate issue,*
" *although she was not prosecuted. The conse-*
" *quence not unfrequently was, that the character*
" *of a woman was sworn away; instances were*
" *known in which, by collusion between the husband*
" *and a pretended paramour, the character of the*
" *wife has been destroyed. All this could take*

" *place, and yet the wife had no defence; she was*
" *excluded from Westminster-hall, and behind her*
" *back, by the principles of our jurisprudence, her*
" *character was tried between her husband and the*
" *man called her paramour.*"

If an English wife be guilty of infidelity, her
husband can divorce *her* so as to marry again;
but she cannot divorce the husband *a vinculo*,
however profligate he may be. No law court
can divorce in England. A special Act of Parliament annulling the marriage, is passed for each
case. The House of Lords grants this almost as
a matter of course to the husband, but not to the
wife. In only four instances (two of which were
cases of incest), has the wife obtained a divorce
to marry again.

She cannot prosecute for a libel. Her husband must prosecute; and in cases of enmity
and separation, of course she is without a
remedy.

She cannot sign a lease, or transact responsible
business.

She cannot claim support, as a matter of personal right, from her husband. The general belief and nominal rule is, that her husband is
" bound to maintain her." That is not the law.
He is not bound to *her*. He is bound to his

country; bound to see that she does not cumber the parish in which she resides. If it be proved that means sufficient are at her disposal, from relatives or friends, her husband is quit of his obligation, and need not contribute a farthing: even if he have deserted her; or be in receipt of money which is hers by inheritance.

She cannot bind her husband by any agreement, except through a third party. A contract formally drawn out by a lawyer,—witnessed, and signed by her husband,—is *void in law*; and he can evade payment of an income so assured, by the legal quibble that "a man cannot contract with his own wife."

Separation from her husband by consent, or for his ill usage, does not alter their mutual relation. He retains the right to divorce her *after* separation,—as before,—though he himself be unfaithful.

Her being, on the other hand, of spotless character, and without reproach, gives her no advantage in law. She may have withdrawn from his roof knowing that he lives with "his "faithful housekeeper": having suffered personal violence at his hands; having "condoned" much, and being able to prove it by unimpeachable testimony: or he may have shut the doors

of her house against her: all this is quite imma-
terial: the law takes no cognisance of which is
to blame. As *her husband*, he has a right to all
that is hers: as *his wife*, she has no right to
anything that is his. As her husband, he may
divorce her (if truth or false swearing can do
it): as his wife, the utmost " divorce " she could
obtain, is permission to reside alone,—married
to his name. The marriage ceremony is a civil
bond for him,—and an indissoluble sacrament
for her; and the rights of mutual property which
that ceremony is ignorantly supposed to confer,
are made absolute for him, and null for her.

Of course an opposite picture may be drawn.
There are bad, wanton, irreclaimable women, as
there are vicious, profligate, tyrannical men: but
the difference is *this:* that to punish and restrain
bad wives, there are laws, and very severe laws
(to say nothing of social condemnation); while
to punish or restrain bad husbands, there is, in
England, no adequate law whatever. Indeed,
the English law holds out a sort of premium on
infidelity; for there is no doubt that the woman
who is divorced for a lover and marries him,
suffers less (except in conscience) than the
woman who *does not deserve to suffer at all*—the
wife of a bad husband, who can inflict what he

pleases, whether she remain in her home, or attempt to leave it.

Such, however, is "the law": and if anything could add to the ridicule, confusion, and injustice of its provisions, it would be the fact, that though it is law for the rich, it is not law for the poor; and though it is the law in England, it is not the law in Scotland!

It is not law for the poor.

Since the days of King Henry VIII., for whose passions it was contrived, our method of divorce has remained an indulgence sacred to the aristocracy of England. The poorer classes have no form of divorce amongst them. The rich man makes a new marriage, having divorced his wife in the House of Lords: his new marriage is legal; his children are legitimate; his bride occupies, in all respects, the same social position as if he had never previously been wedded. The poor man makes a new marriage, *not* having divorced his wife in the House of Lords; his new marriage is null; his children are bastards; and he himself is liable to be put on his trial for bigamy: the allotted punishment for which crime, at one time was hanging, and is now imprisonment. Not always offending knowingly,—for nothing can exceed the ignorance of the poor on this subject; they believe a Magistrate can divorce them; that an absence of seven years constitutes a nullity of the marriage tie; or that they can give each other reciprocal permission to divorce: and among some of our rural populations, the grosser belief prevails, that a man may legally *sell* his wife, and so break the bond of union! They believe anything,--rather than what is the fact,---viz., that *they* cannot do legally, that which they know is done legally in the classes above them; that the comfort of the rich man's home, or the indulgence of the rich man's passions, receives a consideration in England which the poor need not expect to obtain.

It is not the law of Scotland. In your Majesty's kingdom, nothing but

" The rapid running of the silver Tweed "

divides that portion of the realm where women are protected by law,—from that portion where they are *un*protected, though living under the same Sovereign and the same government!

When, in Queen Anne's reign, the legislative union of Scotland was completed, the laws relating to trade, customs, and excise, were assimilated to those of England; but other laws remained untouched; and in nothing is there a larger difference than in all matters relating to marriage, divorce, and legitimation of children.

In Scotland, the wife accused of infidelity defends herself as a matter of course, and as a first process,—instead of suffering by the infamous English action for " damages," where she is not allowed to interfere, though the result may be to ruin her.

In Scotland, the property of the wife is protected; rules are made for her " aliment" or support; and her clothes and " paraphernalia " cannot be seized by her husband.

In Scotland, above all, the law *has* power to divorce *a vinculo*, so as to enable *either* party to marry again; and the right of the wife to apply for such divorce is equal with the right of the husband; that license for inconstancy, taken out under the English law by the English husband,—as one of the masculine gender,—being utterly unknown to the Scottish courts.

———

This condition of the English law; its anomalies, its injustice, its actions for damages and crim. con., and its perpetual contradictions, have long marked it out for reform. At various times, and on various occasions, it has been pronounced,—not by wailing, angry, and complaining women, but by *men*,—senators and judges,—to be " barbarous "—" indecent "—" oppressive "—" anomalous and preposterous "—" utterly disgraceful." When the Marriage Reform Bill was brought in, the late Lord Beaumont stigmatised the examinations before the House of Lords in divorce cases, as "*disgusting and demoralising.*" Lord Campbell spoke of passing Bills of Divorce through the two Houses of Parliament as a "*scandalous practice.*" Lord St. Leonards, while he affirmed that no measure would be satisfactory, that did not reconcile the conflict of our jurisdiction with the Scottish law, declared the present English action for " damages" to be a "*disgrace to the country*"—" *a* " *stigma on the law of England*"—" *an action* " *which shocked one's sense of what was right.*" Lord Brougham,—so long as sixteen years ago, —spoke of the law as regards a woman's earnings in this most forcible language,—" *Could* " *anything be more harsh or cruel,*" he said, " *than that the wife's goods and chattels should* " *be at the mercy of the husband, and that she* " *might work and toil for an unkind father to* " *support his family and children, while the*

c

" *husband repaid her with harshness and bru-*
" *tality, he all the time rioting and revelling in*
" *extravagance and dissipation, and squander-*
" *ing in the company of guilty paramours the*
" *produce of her industry? The law was silent*
" *to the complaints of such a woman.*"

In short, the gentlemen of England—members
of both Houses—have severally denounced in
the most unmeasured terms, the present laws
for women; and unanimously agreed that they
ought to be reformed. Commissioners were
accordingly " ordered to report," and they re-
ported. Lord Cranworth undertook to bring in
the measure which was to set all to rights; and
after some delay, he presented a bill, with his
plan for future alterations. Any one would
have imagined, after the decided admissions of
evil on the part of all concerned, that this bill
would have proposed some sweeping change;
the establishment of a judicial tribunal, as in
Scotland and France, which should have *complete power* in matrimonial causes; and better
laws of protection for women. Not at all. The
gist of the new bill, was simply to take away
power from the Ecclesiastical Courts, and trans-
fer it to the Court of Chancery. It was full of
contradictions. It professed to deprive the House

of Lords of the power of granting divorces, and yet made the House of Lords the court of appeal " *en dernier ressort,*" from the proposed new tribunal. It proposed to "leave the law as it stood," with regard to the right of the wife to apply for divorce; and, in reality, created a new, definite, and anomalous limit; for whereas at present the power of *applying for* (if not of *obtaining*) a Divorce Act, exists for all women who conceive themselves wronged—the Chancellor proposed to classify what were insupportable wrongs, and grant the remedy only to such women as could plead them. Stripped of confusion and technicalities, the object of the bill was simply this; to make it statute law, (instead of Parliamentary practice, as at present,) that marriage should be dissoluble in England; that husbands should divorce their wives, but not wives their husbands; and that the richer class should have the benefit of their riches, by the process remaining comparatively expensive. Only that all this was to be arranged by a different and more decent method. The bill was discussed; opposed; and withdrawn. No lawyer, of whatever eminence, ever yet proposed a measure in either House of Parliament, that all the other lawyers did not rise one by one to tell him that they " objected to the machinery of his bill," and that its provisions were " wholly impracticable." They did so on the present occasion. In one thing only they generally agreed, they congratulated Lord Cranworth upon that portion of his plan which provided that Justice should have her scales ready weighted in favour of the stronger party—viz., that women should by no means be discouraged from forgiving their husbands, by enacting that adultery in the male sex should he considered a ground of divorce—" as in Scotland."

It is with timid reluctance, that I permit myself to allude to the social condition of that unhappy country. To all loyal minds it must be matter for grave and sorrowful reflection, that while your Majesty is surrounded with faithful wives and discreet ladies in London,— Windsor,—and Osborne,—the less cautious portion of the realm in which Balmoral is situated, is plunged in the grossest immorality. England is virtuous; but Scotland is " a hot-bed of vice." It is a land dedicated to Cupid. Statues of Venus are set up in all the principal squares of Edinburgh. The marriage-tie is a mere true lovers' knot. The ladies who present themselves at Holyrood are triumphant Messalinas. And

on the decks of the emigrant vessels which crowd
the harbour of Leith, groups of melancholy cast-
off husbands may be seen, bidding reproachful
farewell to that inhospitable country where they
only exist to be repudiated!

The Scotch ladies will deny their guilt. They
will deny that the upper classes of their nation
have proved themselves more immoral than the
upper classes in England. But they are contradicted by the Lord Chancellor and the whole
house of English Peers. That body of senators
have pronounced, that to permit women in England to have the privilege accorded to the women
of Scotland, would be productive of the grossest
immorality and of multitudinous divorce. Now,
to support that position, one of three things
must be capable of proof. Either, having witnessed the effect of the Divorce Laws of Scotland,—and perceiving its women to be a nation
of lost creatures,—English legislators refuse to
copy those laws, lest English women become as
profligate as Scotch women; or else (and this is
a reason to be carefully considered) they fear to
trust English women with a privilege which their
colder Caledonian sisters are less likely to abuse:
or, lastly, the extreme and universal profligacy
of English husbands, leads them to dread,

that if English women could once obtain the
same privilege of divorce, which is accorded to
Scotch women, two Englishmen out of three
would immediately be discarded by their helpmates; in that startling proportion recorded by
Sir Walter Scott in his poem of the Bridal of
Triermain:—

> " And still these lovers' faith survives,
>   Their truth so constant shewn ;
>   There were two who loved their neighbour's wives,
>   And ONE—who loved his own."

Oh! is it not a sad and marvellous thing, that
professional prejudice. and the prejudice of sex,
can so warp and bend high and honourable minds,
that a man like Lord Cranworth, in Lord Cranworth's position,—the most responsible for justice in England;—should take the view Lord
Cranworth took—to use the arguments Lord
Cranworth used—in support of what? In support of a measure to *legalise* a special indulgence
to the animal passions of men.

Lord Campbell, when some doubt is expressed
whether divorce ought to be permitted at all, to
either sex, rises and says divorce of the wife is
" in accordance with Scripture." In what portion of Holy Writ does he find it in " accordance

with Scripture " that adultery is no sin in a man? Are not men warned not only against sin, but even against wandering desires? For whom is the text—" Whoso looketh on a woman to lust after her, hath already committed adultery with her in his heart"? Or to whom was the reproach addressed—" For the hardness of your hearts Moses gave you this law"? Are we to have one religion for women and another for men, as we have already one law for women and another for men,—ecclesiastical law for the woman, and common law for the man?

The holy Roman Catholic rule is, that marriage is indissoluble for either party. *That* rule all can understand and reverence. But that marriage should be dissoluble for one sex only, and only for the wealthy of that sex; that it should be made a sacrament for the poor and for women, and a civil contract for gentlemen,—who is to understand *that*?

Roman Catholic countries are governed by one general rule; but your Majesty governs a kingdom " divided against itself." Split up into different forms of religious dissent, and the law following that dissent into holes and corners; so that justice becomes a sort of game of hide and seek, and they who find her, light upon her by chance.. Your Majesty's subjects north and south of the Tweed are all "at sixes and severis" as to what should be the law. Yet they are all the subjects of one Queen; the English ladies whom no amount of ill-usage can divorce, and the Scotch ladies who can divorce so easily. Nay, *in the same family* different persons find themselves under different laws. I am myself united to one member of a family in which there are five marriages; in two of which, (being Scotch marriages), the right of divorce would be equal, —while three (being English marriages) could only be dissolved in favour of the husband, and by Act of Parliament. Here, then, are five of your Majesty's subjects, born in one home; of the same parents: and three of the brood are drafted off to be under the English law,—and two to be under Scotch laws, which contradict the English law in every particular! Is that, or is it not, a ridiculous state of things to exist in any kingdom?

But as if that did not make the grotesque confusion sufficiently obvious, it appears that even south of the Tweed, your Majesty's Peers and Commons cannot in the least agree among themselves what is, or ought to be, the law with respect to marriage!

Lord Hardwicke's Marriage Act, of 1754, declared null, all marriages not celebrated by a
priest in orders: and made it indispensable that
the ceremony should take place in some parish
church, or public chapel, unless by special license
from the Archbishop of Canterbury. But Lord
John Russell's Act, of 1836, permits persons, on
the contrary, to be married according to any
form they choose; they need never see a church
or a priest; but by merely repairing to the
" Registrar," giving certain notices, and procur-
ing certain certificates, they acquire a right to
have the ceremony performed, in places regis-
tered and appropriated for the purpose.

More recently, Lord Redesdale,—speaking on
the Lord Chancellor's Bill,—says he shall oppose
any divorce law, and considers marriage should
be " indissoluble :" But Lord St. Leonards
affirms, that " it won't do at this time of day"
to speak of the indissoluble nature of marriage;
and that the only question is, what shall be the
machinery of the new law for its dissolution?
Lord Clancarty (an Irishman) complains that
Ireland is not mentioned in the bill, and speaks
of marriage as a "divine ordinance." But Lord
Campbell (a Scotchman) pooh-poohs the idea of
its being a divine ordinance, and says that mar-

riage was held indissoluble *in times of Popery*, but is not held so *now*; and on that very account a judicial instead of an ecclesiastical jurisdiction ought now to be established. While Mr. Phinn, in the other House, thus clearly defines the position laid down by Lord Campbell:—" An " important alteration has been made in the law " of the country. Up to a recent period it had " been a question agitated by lawyers, whether " marriage was not a religious contract, requir- " ing the sanction of the church. That question " has been settled by the Legislature, and mar- " riage is now a Civil Contract."

Lord Redesdale,—reluctantly succumbing to the Chancellor's " civil contract " views,—thinks, at least, divorce should not be made too cheap, as it would then become too common; on which, Lord Brougham (who many a day of his long energetic life, has stood sentinel to guard the rights of the people), shrewdly enquires whether his lordship means that the proposed new divorce law " shall not apply to 19-20ths of the inhabit- " ants of this country, but only to the 1-20th who " can afford to pay for it?"

Then your Majesty's Lord High Chancellor defines it as *his* opinion, that divorce *a vinculo* should remain moderately expensive, and be

granted *only to husbands;*—but can he convince
your Majesty's Lord High Chamberlain, the
Marquis of Breadalbane, and the Scotch Peers
who come from the other side of the Tweed,
where the law is precisely reversed in both those
particulars?

Finally, Lord Clancarty says, if there *must* be
a law of divorce, he cannot for the life of him
see how we can establish a distinction between
the sin of the man and the woman, which never
was established by divine law;—while the Bishop
of Oxford, religiously ignoring Lord John Russell's Bill of 1836, Lord Cranworth's opinion,
Lord Campbell's explanation, and the actual law
of the northern portion of your Majesty's dominions,—says he shall move to omit all the
clauses of the Bill countenancing *any* divorce
whatever.

And at the end of this confused skirmish of
opinions, the Bill drops, and is given up; the
Chancellor, like the Runic sorceress, exclaims,—

"Leave me, leave me, to repose:"

and all go away home; like a party of miners
who have given up the attempt to dig out persons buried in superincumbent earth! They
would be very glad to do something towards

amending the laws for women, but really "the "subject is so surrounded with difficulty."

Why is it so surrounded with difficulty? Why is England the only country obliged to confess she cannot contrive to administer justice to women? Why is it more difficult than in France? Why more difficult than in Scotland? Simply because our legists and legislators insist on binding tares with wheat, and combining all sorts of contradictions which they never will be able satisfactorily to combine. They never *will* satisfy, with measures that give one law for one sex and the rich, and another law for the other sex and the poor. Nor will they ever succeed in acting on the legal fiction that married women are "non-existent," and man and wife are still "one," in cases of alienation, separation, and enmity; when they are about as much "one" as those ingenious twisted groups of animal death we sometimes see in sculpture; one creature wild to resist, and the other fierce to destroy.

Nor does all this confusion arise, because the law is professedly too weak for the necessary control which would prevent it. The law is strong enough when it interferes with labour,— with property,—with the guardianship of children,—with the rights of speculative industry. We find no difficulty in controlling the merchant in his factories, the master with his apprentices, nor in the protection of persons in all other dependant positions. We find no difficulty in punishing the abuse of power, or discovered crime. It suffices that it be proved that wrong was committed, and punishment follows as a matter of course.

The poor cabin boy is on the high seas. The steward, or the captain, or a brutal messmate, maltreats the boy. He is bruised,—he is maimed, —he is miserable,—that meagre shuffling overworked lad, whose very surname perhaps nobody knows: some little outcast Tom, Jack, or Jim, sent to sea by the parish. Is there no law for *him*? Is it "*so surrounded with difficulty*" that no punishment shall reach those who maltreated him? Read the police report. Though that life seemed as unimportant as a grain of sand, it is cared for. The Spirit of Justice moved with that ship "over the face of the waters," and English law and public government avenge him, who perhaps had not one private friend in the world.

The wandering pedlar trudges over the moor —his pack is heavy; his step is slow; he is dogged by some villain who saw him rest by the way-side inn. He is two hundred miles away from his real home. He came from the thrifty North, and will plod back there with his savings. Return ? No! he will never return. The sharp knife is out—his blood sinks in the short turf where the moorland sheep have been feeding; his moan is lost on the midnight breeze; and his pack is stolen. Is there no law for *him* ? Go and listen in the assize court. There, in the hot glow of summer, amid the buzz of insects and voices, and the loud oratory of declaiming men, you will hear the stillness of that murderous night described; and how its silence and darkness, and the lonely stretch of the apparently deserted heath, failed to shield the modern Cain from the observation of that one " chance witness," whom God seems ever to leave standing sentinel to watch for undiscovered crime. Who would have thought the treasure of that poor pedlar's pack was worth two men's lives ? Yet one was taken by murder, and now this other is forfeited to Justice ; to prove — that the poorest of the Queen's subjects shall not wander on her highways without the same protection of life and property, that guards the fringed canopy of a duke's bed !

Protection for life and property. Is that all ?

Is happiness nothing? Is reputation nothing?
Is the law only able to ward off the assassin's
knife, or make restitution of stolen coin? Is it
able to protect the poorest, the meanest, the
most apparently helpless persons in the realm,
and not able to protect women? Are the only
laws in England "so surrounded with difficulty"
that they cannot possibly be re-modelled to any
pattern of equal justice, the laws between man
and wife?

I think not. I think if men would approach
them with the same impartial wish to make rules
of protection, that is brought to bear on other
subjects, they would find the same facility in
applying those rules.

Now, with respect to the condition and effect
of the laws for women in Scotland, it came out
incidentally in the debate on the Marriage Bill,
that the total amount of all the divorces in that
misguided country, during the last five years,
only averaged twenty in all classes; and this was
not stated in defence of Scotch morality, but as
a means of calculating what might be expected
in England under a new system.

In Scotland, then, though the right of divorce
be *equal*,—and the process so easy that even if
the party accused left the kingdom, he or she

could still be proceeded against by what was termed " edictal citation,"—(or reading the citation aloud at the market-cross of Edinburgh, and the pier and shore of Leith), an average of twenty couples only, availed themselves of the law, the existence of which so alarms English legislators.

Very sparing, indeed, are the cases recorded as disputed precedents. Towards the end of the last century the Duchess of Hamilton divorced the Duke, as a Scotchman, though married by English ritual in England. In 1810, Lady Paget divorced Lord Paget, though he pleaded a reconciliation after his original desertion. In 1813, Catherine Pollock divorced Russell Manners, for desertion for ten years and infidelity. Previous to which cases, Sir T. Wallace Dunlop had the singular good fortune of being proceeded against for divorce by both his first and second wife. The first wife succeeded; but the second failed; not for want of proof of his misconduct, but because her marriage was held to be *an English marriage*, and so, indissoluble by the Scotch Courts.

It is expressly stated that the number of Scotch cases in proportion to the population, remained nearly the same at all periods, since

the Commissioners were appointed in 1563 down
to the present time; and that the conjugal relation "stood not less, but infinitely more sacred
"and secure in Scotland" since total divorce was
made possible, in lieu of separation under ecclesiastical law. Indeed, it will scarcely be urged
that it is a more favourable condition *for morality*,
that a woman should remain for life nominally
married to a man who has deserted her (as under
the English law), than that she should have
power to divorce him and marry again, as under
the Scotch law.

But Lord Chancellor Cranworth argued the
question in a very singular manner; and I give
his argument as it stands in the printed report
of the debate of June 14, 1854:—First, as to the
lighter causes of divorce, admitted in Scotland,
he says:—

" If marriages could be dissolved for cruelty or desertion,
" the husband may dissolve his marriage whenever he pleases ;
" *he has only to be tyrannical to his wife, or to desert her, to*
" *effect the very object he has in view.* Therefore I do not at all
" propose to alter what has been—I will not say the law,—
" because in point of fact there has been no law—but the
" practice on this subject."

Then, as to that graver interruption of domestic quiet, inconstancy, he says:—

" If adultery on the part of the husband is to entitle him
" to a divorce,—inasmuch as the husband (which may be bad
" morality, but it is the fact) suffers little on that account in
" the opinion of the world at large (for it is notorious that,
" while the wife who commits adultery loses her station in
" society, that punishment is not awarded to the husband who
" is guilty of the same crime) *he may, without any great sacri-*
" *fice on his own part, but by merely being a little profligate,* get
" rid of his wife whenever he chooses to do so."

And Lord Campbell, in a subsequent debate,
July 1, strikes out another suggestion; *he* objects
to granting divorces to women, on account of
the ease with which adultery in the husband is
(or ought to be) forgiven by the wife!

" He thought his noble and learned friend had wisely ab-
" stained from following the example of *Scotland and other*
" *countries,* in which the wife had a right to have the mar-
" riage dissolved on account of the adultery of the husband.
" The moral guilt incurred by the husband was the same,—
" but in most cases it might be CONDONED."

In short, what between their dread of en-
couraging the husband to be " a little profligate,"
in order to get rid of his wife,—and fear of in-
clining the wife to be unforgiving, in the pros-
pect of getting rid of her husband,—they think
it best that justice should be not merely impro-

bable, as at present, but made utterly *impossible* for the woman to obtain.

Again I say, it is perfectly marvellous what clever and honourable men will say and do when blinded by strong prejudice! Here are these two great lawyers talking as though the divorce of the husband could be made compulsory on the wife, or dependant on her simple resolution. *Is the wife, after all, to be her own judge?* No; the judge is her judge; the Lord Chancellor himself is her judge; the House of Lords is her judge. The possibility of *applying* for a divorce *a vinculo*, does not suddenly invest her with an authority like that of the patriarch Abraham, to send forth her husband, like weeping Hagar, into the desert world. She is to apply for her divorce to the judicial tribunal : to that Chancellor who speaks of an adulterous husband as being " a " little profligate :" to that House of Lords which has entertained feminine applications with so much jealousy and reluctance, that there have been but four cases (two of them cases of incest), in which the wife's petition for divorce has ever been granted. With these judges, and not with the wife, rests the decision whether she has refused that indulgence which ought to be a part of her nature, and is the principal charm of her sex,

—or whether, wronged, outraged, and forsaken, she has borne to the last verge of endurance before she appealed to the law! With these judges, and not with the wife, remains the great decree which shall pronounce whether " condon-" ation " was or was not absolutely impossible, under the circumstances she pleads as her argument for liberty.

No doubt, in numberless instances, condonation *is* possible. So far we will grant Lord Cranworth's argument. A man may yield to the temptation of passion, who yet at heart loves and respects his wife; and feels, after his delusion is over, a real shame and repentance. Nor is want of chastity the only sin in the world;—a woman who is a chaste wife may fill her husband's days with unendurable bitterness; and a man who has lapsed in his observance of the marriage vow, may nevertheless be a kindly husband and father, with whom reconcilement would be a safe and blessed generosity. If we add to these admissions, woman's natural lingering love for her companion; love undeniable; indisputable; love evidenced each day, even among the poor creatures who come bruised and bleeding before the police courts; refusing to give evidence, in a calmer hour, against the man such evidence would condemn to punishment : if we add the love of children; the dread of breaking the bond which shall perhaps help a step-mother into the mother's vacated place: if we add the obvious interest, in almost every instance, which the woman has to remain in her home; and the horror most women must feel at the idea of the public exposure and discussion of such wrongs; it is evident they would not be so very eager to avail themselves, *in usual cases*, of the extreme remedy.

But in *un*usual cases—in cases of the dreary, stormy, deserted life—where profligacy, personal violence, insult, and oppression, fill up the measure of that wrong which pardon cannot reach, —why is there to be no rescue for the woman? Why is such a man to be sheltered under the Lord Chancellor's term of "only a little profligate,"—and "condonation" be supposed the only proper notice of his conduct?

While the laws that women appeal to, are administered by men, we need not fear that their appeals will be too carelessly granted. No statement can be more incontrovertible than the Lord Chancellor's *dictum*, that the profligate husband "suffers little in the opinion of the world at large." It were well if he were held harmless

only by public opinion : but he is also held harmless by LAW.

In the very session during which Lord Cranworth's Bill was discussed, some remarkable cases
occurred, both in the upper and lower classes;
some of which were public, and some not. I
give the latter, therefore, without the names. It
is enough for me, that your Majesty knows these
cases *did* occur; and this record of what the
English law was, in your Majesty's reign, will
remain,—when the names shall signify no more
than the N. or M. in the Church Catechism.

In the upper classes, a young peer deserted his
young wife (then near her confinement of her
first child), informing her as his reason for doing
so, that he had always preferred his mistress, to
whom he should now return, and bid his wife
farewell for ever.

In that case, whether by the interference of
friends, or the generosity and discretion of the
" condoning" wife, a reconciliation was effected :
but had this desirable event not taken place, the
law of England is as follows :—

This young deserted wife, not yet a mother,
would remain as much the wife of her deserting
husband, as if they were the happiest couple that
ever honey-mooned under one roof. She did

well to "condone," for she was utterly at his
mercy. If, in the course of the long years of
loneliness which her future was to bring, the
husband imagined there was anything in *her*
conduct which might bear evil construction, he
had the same right to divorce her he had
before they parted; but she could not divorce
him. Under no circumstances,—of libel, insult,
or attempt to defame her without cause,—though
he added half a dozen mistresses to the first,
could *she* break her marriage with *him*. He
would have the right, for any number of years,
to dog her from place to place, sending attorneys
to "make enquiries" at all her places of residence, calculated to slur her reputation, even if
he succeeded in nothing more. Her pleading
his desertion, or their separation, would not bar
his right. The English law takes no cognisance
of separations, and does not divorce for the
husband's adultery and desertion, as in Scotland. Neither (unless by special settlement,
contract through third parties, or suit for
alimony following a suit in the Ecclesiastical
Courts) would he be bound to support her, or
pay any debt of hers, if she had an income of
her own, sufficient without his aid. She could
not marry any other man; but must remain, as

the Lord Chancellor thinks it just that women should remain in such cases, married *to the name* of the husband, who has free leave, in law, to forsake her, spend his fortune on his mistress, or mistresses, watch his opportunity (if possible) to divorce *her*, and "suffering little in the opinion of the world at large," remain, himself, triumphantly, undivorceable through life! In an instance of desertion some years ago, the husband lived at an hotel, calling his mistress by his wife's name, and took lodgings for her in his wife's name, with perfect impunity. Where was the remedy? There was none.

A second case last session, was one in which a married man of rank came to England, to dispute the guardianship of an infant child born of a double adultery; the married lady who was its mother having been divorced for his sake. The evil bond between them being already broken, each desired to retain this "pledge of love," the person of the little child. It was seized by the mother; regained by the father; made the subject of police struggles on the Continent, and of a threatening scandal in England. What the law would have decided in that wonderful case, of a man coming to claim under the law, a child born out of the law, from the hapless mother

who had already suffered irreparable wrong and
degradation on account of its birth,—I do not
know; but this I *do* know, that this claimant
of his illegitimate child has the same right, under
the English law, to the guardianship of his
legitimate children, as any other husband would
have: a right to interfere with their possession
by his wife,—though his legitimate children are
girls; and his open claim of his illegitimate child,
and his having been the public cause of the
divorce of its mother, gives his wife no right
whatever to divorce *him* "*a vinculo*"; nor is
there the remotest possibility, under the English
law, of breaking her marriage. His wife she is;
and his wife she must remain, even if she were
never to see him again; and if he were the
father of as many natural children as Charles II.

A third case (to which I shall recur) is my
own: in which, after personal violence, ill-usage,
an "action for damages," and a long separation,
the husband—being desirous to raise money,—
procured a contract to be signed between himself
and his wife, containing certain provisions as to
his trust-funds, and as to her income, both before
and after the death of certain parties. That
contract was witnessed and signed by the husband himself; by the solicitor who drew it up,

—a gentleman distinguished in his own branch of the legal profession: and by the Hon. Edmund Phipps, brother to the Marquis of Normanby, your Majesty's Minister at the Court of Tuscany, and to the Hon. Charles Phipps, Treasurer to the Prince Consort.

When the income so secured (or supposed to be secured), was claimed for creditors, the husband, in this case, refused to pay it. The law of England proved to be, that the wife being " non-existent," or one with the husband, *could not legally make any contract with him.* The signature of the husband, the signature of the brother of those other distinguished persons in your Majesty's service,—and the signature of the lawyer who drew up the agreement,—all failed to make it more valuable than a sheet of blank paper. The wife, who might have compelled the execution of such a contract had she been a menial servant, was left without a remedy, *because she was a wife;* and without further explanation than that "the law" would hold her husband harmless, for mocking her and mocking the gentlemen who had added their signatures, by offering this fictitious security.

In lower life,—occurring as an illustration of the divorce laws for the rich,—a respectable tradesman was tried for bigamy, and convicted. The second wife deposed, that he had courted her for six years; had no money with her; on the contrary, supplied her with money since his apprehension; had always been very kind; and that they had a child of his, residing with them. The undivorced wife was living with an omnibus man, and had been in a lunatic asylum. Mr. Russell Gurney, in deciding the case, observed, with epigrammatic truth, that " this was one of " those unfortunate cases, in which, in the pre- " sent state of the law, *if a man was not pos-* " *sessed of wealth, he had no power to remedy his* " *situation :*" and knowing (as we do know), that if, instead of plain Mr Gray and obscure Mary Adams, these parties had been Lord Grayton and Lady Mary, we should simply have had " Grayton's Divorce Bill" going quietly through the House of Lords, we can scarcely wonder if murmurs arise, against this wonderful system of legislation.

In an old fashioned book (written by a favou- rite of your Majesty's Uncle, George the Fourth), the author says: "if a poor man were " to appear in the lobby of the House of Lords, " praying to be divorced *gratis* from his wife, it " is likely that the Sergeant-at-Arms would take

" him for some poor lunatic, and send him to
" Bedlam; yet I can see no reason why a country-
" man should not be divorced at Quarter Sessions,
" as well as a nobleman in the House of Lords."
Nor I—if divorce is to be allowed at all.

In humble life, again (though no worse off
than if she had been provided for by a contract
bearing the signatures of one of the Metropolitan
Magistrates, and the brother of your Majesty's
Ambassador, and Prince Albert's Treasurer), a
Mrs Adsett claimed support from her husband,
a gun-maker. The husband very coolly informed
the Magistrate that he could not support her;
*on the contrary, for some months she had sup-
ported him;* but she might "come back to him."
The wife replied that he had a mistress, and she
had three children. The magistrates remarked
that they were "very sorry," but the wife must
go "to the home provided for her:"—mistress
or no mistress:—the law of England not making
that a ground of special protection. "Starve,
or condone." Take the children, and go to the
husband, who is "a little profligate,"—and who
is supported by you, that he may spend his
money on his concubine.

That is the language of the law.

It is, however, satisfactory to learn, that

although *women* are not protected in England, *property* is guarded by the most stringent rules; and to balance the indignation we might feel at broken contracts, earnings-wasted on mistresses, and general oppression, we are comforted by knowing that in February, this year, Sir Baldwin Leighton having convicted his gamekeeper of sending a present of two dead rabbits to a person in Shrewsbury, after he had agreed to look after 2,000 acres of land, without perquisites,—the magistrates,—with expressions of regret (several county magistrates coming forward to give the gamekeeper an excellent character), sentenced him to imprisonment, as " guilty of what the law called larceny." And we are further edified by an incidental statement of Lord Brougham (in discussing a bill now pending), that, in 1849, three men, each approaching 70 years of age, were tried at different sessions, in a county, the name of which he would not mention. One was sentenced to six weeks' imprisonment with hard labour, *for stealing to the amount of about* 1*d.*; another to eight weeks' hard labour *for stealing to the amount of* $\frac{1}{2}d.$; and a third to four weeks' hard labour *for stealing to the amount of* $\frac{1}{4}d.$ Nor had he reason to believe that there were any aggravating circumstances in their cases. He knew, indeed, of another case, in a different county, in which a man in his 70th year, was sentenced to *twelve months' imprisonment with hard labour for stealing to the amount of 3d.* But he assumed that in that case there must have been aggravating circumstances.

No " aggravating circumstances," however, on the part of a husband, can bring the law to bear upon *him ;* and while the poor man lies in prison a year, for theft to the value of three pence;— while the gamekeeper, hitherto respected and respectable in his station of life, is consigned, for a briefer term, to the same abode of guilt, for sending two rabbits to a tradesman's kitchen, —the " gentleman," who spends on his mistress the income of his wife, or openly defrauds her on a signed contract,—laughs in the face of justice, and mocks the power of the law.

In brief, the legal axiom is, that sin is not sin in a man, if it be against a woman; and more especially against the woman he vowed at God's altar to cherish and protect. Marriage is, according to the great law authorities in and out of Parliament, not a religious bond, but a civil contract. The religious vow, taken by the man in marriage, is merely to give him civil rights

over the woman "sworn in" as his special wife.
She is bound to afford him every assistance; to
be "true till death"; to be obedient to his will;
and to "condone" his guilty pleasures—and *he*
is bound to nothing at all, except a nominal
union, much resembling in its principle that
singular invention, the Russian "Drosky," in
which we see one horse harnessed within shafts,
and drawing the weight of the carriage, and the
other caracoling and frisking in the most light
agreeable and ornamental manner by its side, but
bearing no part of the restraint imposed.

Mr. Gladstone, speaking on the Marriage
Amendment Bill, says that "when the gospel
"came into the world, woman was elevated to an
"equality with her stronger companion,"—and
that there is "perfect equality between man and
"woman as far as the marriage tie is concerned,"
—and he asks whether it is now "intended to
"have one marriage code for men and another
"for women?" But I say, there is *already* one
marriage code for men and another for women:
and as to the gospel view of woman's position,
—in vain are women pointed out as "the
"last at the cross, and the first at the tomb;" in
vain, one of that humbled sex was made the
mother of the Saviour of mankind; in vain, all

through the gospel pages, their faith, their sorrows, their errors, are held up as obtaining attention and mercy from the divine "Man of "sorrows and acquainted with grief," who wept with the sisters of Lazarus, and comforted the widow of Nain. A sneer is the only answer to Mr. Gladstone's "gospel" doctrine; and the only text on the subject acknowledged by Parliament, is the Old Testament text: "*and he shall rule* "*over her.*" We keep the doctrine of the Fall—not of the Redemption.

There was, indeed, an old-fashioned time when an attempt was made to show legal discouragement to men who were " a little profligate." We read that in the reign of James I. Sir Pecksael Brocas—(probably, by his name, a sinner of Dutch extraction)—"having been convicted of "many notorious adulteries," was made to do penance, by standing in a white sheet at St. Paul's Cross, holding a stick in his hand. But for the most part, the state of law, and of public opinion, has been very much what the Lord Chancellor Cranworth thinks it may fairly remain. If Lord Cranworth goes through that process which the wisest of witty men, and the wittiest of wise men,—the late Sydney Smith,—called " putting *a spine* to history," and connects

the various events of different reigns, it must be
a satisfaction to him to remark, how widely
different has been the measure dealt to sinful
Kings and erring Queens. We trace the incon-
tinence of the former by successive creations
in the peerage; and the faults of the latter,
by records of imprisonment and death on the
scaffold.

What the exact degree of Anne Boleyn's
guilt may have been, accused as she was of
crimes which even at the time no one believed
she had committed:—what the balance of indis-
cretion or vice in that fair Queen of Scots, who
sate in her narrow prison-room in your Majesty's
Palace of Holyrood, embroidering head-dresses
for her vain rival Queen Elizabeth, with a weak
attempt at propitiation:—

What the real history was, of Sophia Dorothea,
—Queen of George I., mother of George II., and
grandmother of Frederick the Great,—who pined
away the years of an English reign, in a Hano-
verian dungeon; parted from her children; having seen the man for whom she was slandered,
die like Rizzio, poniarded and buried under the
floor of her dressing-room: and who yet retained
strength and courage for that noble reply, when
urged to supplicate for a reconciliation:—" *No*

E

" —if I am guilty, I am not worthy to be your
"Queen; if I am innocent, your King is not
"worthy to be my husband:"—

How far Caroline of Brunswick was pre-judged
and fore-doomed, when she came to this country,
to find the Countess of 'Jersey already appointed
her lady-in-waiting, and to be welcomed—not as
a bride, but as a scrip-share, by that indebted
Prince, who had pledged his royal word he was
not already married to Mrs. Fitzherbert:—

What the truth was, in short,—respecting all
or any of these dead Queens,—over whose sense-
less dust contending historians still do battle,—
we can never know.

But *this* we *do* know ; that the punishment,
here, of those sins which have no distinction in
Divine law, was meted very differently to them
and their royal helpmates: that history describes
the tyrant husband of Anne Boleyn, as one
" who never spared man in his wrath, or woman
in his lust:" that the great-grandson of scaffold-
sentenced Mary—the son of scaffold-sentenced
Charles,—popularly known by the name of " the
merry monarch,"—had so many natural children
by various mothers, that they formed quite a
group in the peerage; occupying the Dukedoms
of Monmouth—Southampton—Grafton—North-

umberland—St. Alban's—Somerset—and Richmond;—two of which titles—Grafton and St. Alban's—remain in direct line from Charles, down to the present time. We know, that his court was an example of the most extravagant and unpunished licentiousness: that Sir John Denham and the Earl of Chesterfield were both accused in his reign of poisoning their wives (the latter administering the poison in the wine of the Holy Communion); and that the King's "merry" favorite, the Duke of Buckingham, killed the Earl of Shrewsbury and held a love appointment with the Earl's wife the same evening. We know, that his brother, James II. had, by Mrs. Churchill (sister of the Duke of Marlborough), the Duke of Berwick—the Grand Prior—and others; and, by Mrs. Sedley, a daughter created Countess of Dorchester, and one, divorced from the Earl of Anglesea, who became Duchess of Buckingham. And we know that the husband of the slandered and imprisoned Dorothea of Zell, having married her only for the sake of uniting the dominions of the family, was utterly unfaithful to her; that Madlle. Schulenberg (created Duchess of Kendal)—Madame Kilmanseg—and that "best beloved mistress of the King,"—the beautiful Countess of Platen, afterwards Countess

of Darlington—accompanied him to the England
which his lawful wife was held unworthy to see,
and supplied her place in his affections, and his
royal palaces, while she lived and died in
prison.

This also we know,—that the son of that
mournful queen,—George II., lived as his father
had lived—very cheerfully; and two anecdotes
are related of his court, worthy to be remembered. One, that Mr. Howard, husband of one
of the King's mistresses (afterwards Countess of
Suffolk), went to St. James's Palace, publicly
to demand his wife; and, being thrust out, sent
a letter to her by the Archbishop of Canterbury;
who conveyed the summons *to the* QUEEN, *who
delivered the letter to her rival!* The other
anecdote—equally curious—that when his son,
the Prince of Wales died, the King (who had
been on bad terms with him, and had never
visited him in his last illness) was playing cards
as usual in Lady Yarmouth's apartments. A
page arrived to tell him his son was no more.
He rose without emotion, crossed to Lady Yarmouth's card-table, and leaning over her chair,
said quietly, "Fritz is dead." And this was a
King whose Queen " condoned " everything.

On the details of the history of George IV.'s

queen, no one would desire to dwell. But Dr. Lushington had courage, in pleading her cause, to remark on the ridicule of a man " seeking to " be divorced at the age of sixty, from a wife " from whom he had been twenty-four years " separated, by his own act, and for the gratifi- " cation of his own appetites." Her death did not appease him. The chief Magistrate of London, Sir R. Baker, resigned on account of the King's displeasure at the royal corpse being suffered to pass; and Major-General Sir R. Wilson was removed from the army by royal order, for the part he had taken in the Queen's favour; on which occasion the public feeling was manifested by a public subscription being raised to compensate the General for the loss of his commission, to the extent of £10,000.

" There's such divinity doth hedge a king," that it is rarely their vices find opposition, even in the church. Charlemagne divorced and married nine wives. When Henry VIII. needed divorces, convenient Cranmer and the convocation granted three in succession,—and when the venerable Fisher, Bishop of Rochester, objected to the King's views, he paid for it with his poor remnant of life. His letters are extant, a neglected prisoner in the tower; writing vain appeals, in the dreary month of December, to the secretary of that bloated and triumphant monarch; pleading, not for life or liberty, but that his clothing was so rent that it did not keep him warm, and his diet so slender that he was well nigh starved, being often given food he was too feeble and aged to eat. What then? In that Tower of London we pass as we go down the river to kindly Nell Gwynne's hospital at Greenwich, the weak old bishop was left to starve and shiver through the inclement winter, and was executed in the pleasant month of June: and in a year from that time, the " Defender of the Faith and Father of the Reformation " had cut off the head of his adored Anne Boleyn, and was dressed in white and silver as an exultant bridegroom, to marry a fresher love; declaring the children of his former marriages (our Queen Mary and Queen Elizabeth), to be both bastards.

Other (though less brilliant) examples of the dazzled way in which the vices of great and powerful men are contemplated, might be quoted; of which one is pleasant, on account of the ingenious frivolity of the ground of justification. When, in Luther's time, the Elector of Hesse wanted to unite himself to the Countess de Saal, he assured Luther that his main reason was—

economy: that the extreme expense of the train
of attendant carriages, baggage-waggons, etc.,
necessary when he made progresses through his
electorate with that respected princess his legitimate wife, was really more than the finances of
the country would bear; while with the Countess
de Saal he would feel justified in adopting a
much more simple style of travelling; (an historical warning to woman, against too many impe-
rials!) Luther, like Cranmer, bowed to the
reasoning of his ruler,—and Lord Campbell may
think the Electress could not do better than
"condone"; but I much fear the judges' wives
would be a good deal startled by its being held
reasonable, when their husbands go circuits, that
they and their many travelling trunks should be
superseded in favour of a young lady (if there
be such a young lady), who would content herself with a single bandbox. Society at large,
however, would be satisfied. We have it on the
authority of the Lord Chancellor (and, indeed,
on the evidence of our own experience), that
the profligate husband "suffers little or nothing
in the opinion of the world." The stereotyped
homily for the two sexes is different. To the
man, the law of the land and the law of custom,

speaking by the mouth of the Lord Chief Justice
of England, says thus:—

"Plena indulgentia!" Fear nothing! Let
what will happen, nothing can hurt *you*. Bring
your mistresses into your house, or leave your
home to reside with them. Give your wife's
name to one, and travel about with her under
that profaned designation. You, my poor friend,
shall lose none of your rights as a husband and
father. Your wife may perhaps resent; but I
hope she will rather see the wisdom of "condoning." Your crime is no crime in the eyes
of society; and as to Scripture, the marriage
bond *is only a civil contract;* what have we
lawyers to do with Divine Law? Your wife
ought to forgive you. You have not been guilty
of incest. There is no earthly reason she should
not wait patiently till you are satiated with your
present course of life, and gladly welcome you
back. There is nothing to prevent her pardon-
ing the desertion and persecution of years; even
if you have libelled her reputation, and endeavoured to get rid of her by divorce; by accusing
her of the sin which at heart you knew she was
not guilty of, and you are.

If she were but guilty, and proved so,—then,

indeed, all were easy! To the irrevocable shame, to the inevitable forsaking, to poverty and oblivion—let her pass! it is doom—but it is also justice: it is the mighty arm of the Law which has seized her, and will fling her from the Tarpeian rock of social condemnation, into the dark gulf of overwhelming disgrace.

But if she be blameless: and if, contumacious and resentful, she harshly refuses to "condone"; if, with blind self-will and arrogance, she has the indecent hardihood to resist, and complain. If she wail and worry for JUSTICE, and talk of the mother who loved—the father who sheltered —the brother who will protéct her,—and insist on being "separated" from you and vour mistress,—then, my poor friend, I fear we *must* do something; but we will do as little as possible: we will give her (what, in point of fact, you have already given her), "the Woman's Divorce";—leave to remain ALONE. Alone— married to your name. Never to know the protection of this nominal husband—nor the joys of family—nor the every-day companionship of a real home. Never to feel or show preference for any friend not of her own sex; though tempted, perhaps, by a feeling nobler than passion; gratitude for generous pity, that has lightened the dreary days. To be slandered, tormented, insulted; to find the world, and the world's law, as the Lord Chancellor truly observes, utterly indifferent to her wrongs or her husband's sin; and through all this to lead a chaste, unspotted, patient, cheerful life ; without anger, without bitterness ; and with meek respect for those English edicts which, with a perverse parody on Scripture, pronounce that " it is not good for " MAN to be alone,"—but extremely good for woman. Hard that a husband should not divorce an adulterous wife! Hard that he should not form a " purer connection !" Hard (though *he* has a career and occupations out of his own home), that a second chance of domestic happiness should not again greet him!—But not the least hard that his weaker partner, elevated, according to Mr Gladstone, to an equality with him, since the Christian advent,—she, who if she has not a home has nothing—should be left stranded and wrecked on the barren sands, at the foot of the world's impassive and impassable rocks.

" Oh! she ought to have *condoned*: she ought " to have been quiet: her friends ought to have " hushed it all up."—Perhaps. But there is one other contingency : there is the contingency that

the woman may say: " *Would I had been indeed*
" *a sinner and divorced, rather than live this life*
" *of torment, injustice, and mockery !*" Wild
words: terrible sinful words: are they not? A
bad, shocking woman to say so; nothing of the
saint and martyr in her composition. But also
a bad law I think. A bad, wicked law, which
makes it utterly indifferent whether she can or
can not claim to be an innocent woman: and
whether her husband is or is not a bad worthless
man.

Either let men renounce the privilege of
divorce, and the assertion that marriage is a
dissoluble contract,—or allow the weaker party
that refuge from intolerable wrong, which they
claim as a matter of necessity for themselves.
The Ecclesiastical law, which denies the dissolu-
bility of marriages, is intelligible, (though not
so intelligible how, that being the case, ecclesias-
tics re-marry persons divorced by parliament).
And the Scotch law, which reverses the ecclesiastical law, and makes marriage dissoluble for
both sexes and all classes, is intelligible. But
the Lord Chancellor's Bill, which denies to the
poor what it gives to the rich—and grants to the
husband what it refuses to the wife—is *not* intelligible on any principle of justice.

In denying women the equal claim, which
even the Ecclesiastical Courts admit, as far as
they admit *any* divorce, Lord Cranworth asserts
himself to be wiser than Lord Eldon,—wiser
than Lord Thurlow,—and wiser (which is very
possible) than Lord Rosslyn; for those three
deceased Chancellors, on one and the same occasion, agreed that the principle on which such
claim ought to be admitted was simply this:
where there was an impossiblity of reconciliation.
It is true that the particular case on which that
debate took place, was a case of incest. It was
the first instance of a divorce bill passed in
England on the petition of the wife; in the year
1801; in the case of Mr Addison, who had lived
with the sister of his wife. But the general argument was not limited to that one crime by Lord
Thurlow; and if it had been, what new confusion is to arise, if the bill now pending, for
Marriage with a Deceased Wife's Sister, should
become law? Is Lord Cranworth's exception no
longer to deserve that distinction? Or is it to
remain incest if combined with adultery; and
cease to be incest when combined with marriage?
What is to be the rule?

Lord Thurlow did not attempt to classify, (as
Lord Cranworth has done,) *what* should be held

to be unendurable wrong; he said merely, that he had been excited by the bill to examine the whole subject of divorce, and that he was of opinion the remedy was *not* confined to the husband. That the principle should be,—the impossibility of reconciliation. He said,—" *Why* " *do you grant to the husband a divorce for the* " *adultery of the wife? Because he ought not to* " *forgive; and separation is inevitable. Where* " *the wife cannot forgive,—and separation is in-* " *evitable by reason of the crime of the husband,—* " *the wife is entitled to the like remedy. Why* " *should she be condemned, for* HIS *crime, to spend* " *the rest of her days in the unheard-of situation,* " *of being neither virgin, wife, nor widow?*"

The speech of Lord Thurlow converted Lord Eldon; the principle was admitted by all; and the Bill of Divorce was granted to the complaining wife.

It is impossible previously to define a limit for unendurable wrong, though it be possible to judge a case when heard. By the Scotch law, *desertion* is held to be a sufficient cause; by several of the countries which follow the old Roman law, causes of personal disgust or dislike; this may be erring on the contrary side, and giving too great facility for divorce; but on no principle of common sense can it be fit that there should exist cases of wrong which the law *cannot* judge, for that sets a limit to the possibility of justice.

———

So long as a husband is not guilty of incest,—a wife, (according to Lords Cranworth and Campbell), has nothing to complain of which she might not "*condone.*" Yet God knows it seems difficult to imagine what shade of torment, insult, or injury, could be added to what has been endured in my own case. I have learned the law respecting women, piece-meal, by suffering from every one of its defects of protection. I married very young, and my marriage was an unhappy one. My family interfered earnestly and frequently in my behalf: and as for me, I forgave and resented—resented and forgave—till at length I left my husband's for my sister's house. He wrote then, adjuring me to pardon him; beseeching me, by all that was holy, "not to crush him," but "to trust to him," to return! He said he "*knelt to me for pardon*"! He wrote to my family in the extremest and most exaggerated terms of submission. He said he was glad

they had avenged me and scorned him, and he
vowed to treat me kindly for the future. To my
lasting injury,—(even now I will not write, to
my lasting *regret,)*—I " *condoned.*" I knew I was
not myself faultless; I was deeply touched by
his imploring phrases; and I returned to the
home and the husband I had abjured. My family,
however, did not choose to resume terms of in-
timacy with him; and he quarrelled with me *on
that account.* I insisted on my right to take my
children to my brother's house, though my
brother would not receive him. Those children
were kidnapped while I was with my sister,
and sent by my husband to a woman who has
since left him money, and of whom he knew I
had the worst opinion.

At that time the law was, (and I thank God I
believe I was greatly instrumental in changing
that law), that a man might take children from
the mother at any age, and without any fault or
offence on her part. There had been an instance
in which the husband seized and carried away a
suckling infant, as his wife sate nursing it in her
own mother's house. Another, in which the
husband being himself in prison for debt, gave
his wife's legitimate child to the woman he cohabited with. A third (in which the parties

were of high rank), where the husband deserted his wife; claimed the babe born after his desertion (having already his other children); and left her to learn its death from the newspapers! A fourth, in which the husband living with a mistress, and travelling with her under his wife's name, the latter appealed for a separation to the Ecclesiastical Court; and the adulterous husband, to revenge himself, claimed from her his three infant girls. In all these cases, and in all other cases, the claim of the father *was held to be indisputable.* There was no law then to help the mother, as there is no law now to help the wife. The blamelessness of the mother signified nothing in those days, as the blamelessness of the wife signifies nothing in this present day. The father possessed precisely the right the husband still possesses—namely, to do exactly what he pleased. Mr Norton, then, took my little children (aged two, four, and six years); and I traced them to the house of that vile woman, who threatened to give me " to the police" when I went there and claimed them.

It was not till six weeks *after* the stealing of my children—after a long, angry correspondence —and after having attempted to condition that " if my family would retract all that had been said against *him*, he would retract all he had said against *me*—that Mr Norton took higher ground than his real cause of anger,—and appeared before the world in the character of "an injured husband." He brought an action against Lord Melbourne; who was in no way connected with our quarrel; who had been a most kind friend to us; and with whom, the last time I had ever seen him in my home,—my husband was on the best possible terms, endeavouring to procure from him a loan of money! The infamous opportunity afforded to unscrupulous men, in the English "Action for Damages" (which Lord St Leonard's has lately termed a "*disgrace to the country*"—"*a stigma on the law of England,*"—"*an action which shocks one's sense of what is right*") was suggested as a temptation and a bait. Lord Melbourne declared that, so far as Mr Norton was concerned, he believed the action to be brought entirely as a means of obtaining money. And, as to the persons who were known to have instigated the proceedings, he considered it was a political plot on the part of a small section of the Tories, to ruin him as Prime Minister. And I know that in this opinion your Majesty's Uncle, King William IV., entirely concurred.

F

Lord Melbourne never for a moment supposed
Mr Norton was *really* jealous of him; but scornfully wrote to me thus,—of my husband,—"*You*
" *ought to know him better than I do, and must do*
" *so. But you seem to me to be hardly aware*
" *what a* GNOME *he is. In my opinion he has*
" *somehow or other made this whole matter subser-*
" *vient to his pecuniary interest.*"

I do not know what pecuniary advantage
consenting to bring the lost trial obtained for
Mr Norton: though if he had won it, certainly
the " damages " would have been excessive;
Lord Melbourne being represented by Mr Norton's counsel, as a profligate old grandee, who
had come into this happy home, to seduce the
youthful and beloved mother of Mr Norton's
three infant children. I do not know, I say,
what base bargain may have been made about
it, as Lord Melbourne conjectured there was;
but this I believe, that but for the scheme to
oust Lord Melbourne as a Minister, and the
feasibility of an action for " damages," this
quarrel with my husband might have been
arranged—as other disputes had been, equally
bitter.

At the trial, it was proved that the witnesses
for the " injured husband " had received money,

and had actually resided till the time of trial at
the country-seat of Lord Grantley, Mr Norton's
elder brother. The jury listened with incredulity
and disgust to the evidence; and without re-
quiring to hear a single witness for Lord Melbourne, or leaving the jury-box, they instantly
gave their verdict against Mr Norton: a verdict
which was received with cheers which the judge
could not suppress: so vehement was the ex-
pression of public contempt and indignation.

Mr David Leahy thus described the feeling of
the time:—" *All the world—whatever their poli-*
" *tics may be, or whatever their opinions about*
" *the discretion of the behaviour of all or either*
" *of the three principal parties—must acknow-*
" *ledge that the three principal witnesses were*
" *perjured and suborned. I have spoken with*
" *almost every person present, and there exists a*
" *perfect unanimity upon this point.*"

After the trial was over, Mr Norton notified
to me that my family might support me, or that
I might write for my bread; and that my children were by law at his sole disposal.

And here, again, MONEY was his avowed motive; for he first affirmed that the residence of
these infants with me would make him liable
for the debts of my household; and then, that

"others" on whom he himself depended, would not permit him to send back his children, as it would appear to justify me, and so prove the trial a mockery.

His own counsel, Sir John Bayley, gave this account in a published letter last year:—" I " found Mrs Norton anxious only on one point, " and nearly broken-hearted about it; namely, the " restoration of her children. She treated her " pecuniary affairs as a matter of perfect indif- " ference, and left me to arrange them with Mr " Norton as I thought fit. I found her husband, " on the contrary, anxious ONLY about the pecuni- " ary arrangement, and so obviously making the " love of the mother for her offspring a means of " barter and bargain, that I wrote to him I could " be ' no party to any arrangement which made " Money the price of Mrs Norton's fair and " honourable access to her children.' I found the " taking away of those children had been the real " ground of quarrel; and that not only Mr Norton " threw the blame of the subsequent trial on his " advisers, and declared that the trial was brought " ' against his judgment,' but that one of his angri- " est grounds of complaint against his wife was, that " she had said she 'never would return to him.' . . . " I found, under Mr Norton's own handwriting,

" *confessions of the grossest personal violence to-*
" *wards his wife.* . . . *Mr Norton admitted to me*
" *his firm belief of his wife's innocence of the*
" *charge he had brought against her and Lord*
" *Melbourne.* . . . *I consider there never was a*
" *more deeply-injured woman, and that his con-*
" *duct to her certainly had been marked by ' the*
" *grossest cruelty, injustice, and inconsistency,' that*
" *ever any man displayed.*"

One of my children was afterwards killed, for
want of the commonest care a mother would
have given to her household. Mr Norton allowed
this child to lie ill a week before he sent to tell
me he was dying; and, when I arrived, I found
the poor little creature already in his coffin.

When it was not a case of death, I was not
allowed to hear at all. Once, when they were
ill, I wrote to ask news of them; and my own
letter was refolded and sent back to me. That
husband, whose petition for pardon had touched
me so easily, never pitied *me*. What I suffered
respecting those children, God knows, and He
only: what I endured, and yet lived past,—of
pain, exasperation, helplessness, and despair,
under the evil law which suffered any man, for
vengeance or for interest, to take baby children
from the mother, I shall not even try to explain.

I believe *men* have no more notion of what that anguish is, than the blind have of colours; and I bless God that at least mine was *one* of the cases which called attention to the state of the law as it then existed.

After the action against Lord Melbourne (in which, according to the preposterous English code, I could have *no personal defence*, nor any means of showing how I had been treated as a wife); I consulted counsel whether *I* could not now divorce my husband: whether a divorce " by reason of cruelty" might not be pleaded for me; and I laid before my lawyers the many instances of violence, injustice, and ill-usage, of which the trial was but the crowning example. I was then told that no divorce *I* could obtain would break my marriage; that I could not plead cruelty *which I had forgiven;* that by re-turning to Mr Norton I had " *condoned* " all I complained of. I was an ENGLISH WIFE, and for me there was no possibility of redress. The answer was always the same. The LAW. " Have I no remedy?"—" No remedy in LAW. The LAW "can do nothing for you: your case is one of " singular, of incredible hardship; but there is "no possible way in which the LAW could assist "you." I tried the Edinburgh lawyers. I in-

quired if they could not prove my marriage a
Scotch one, all Mr Norton's property being in
Scotland, his father a Scotch Baron of Exchequer,
and his mother of a Scotch family,—but without
success.

When the woman died, to whom my children
had been sent, Mr Norton proposed to me to
" forgive " the public trial, and return to him
(showing how much *he* had believed its accusations). I received from him a most extraordinary
note, saying that he considered our differences
" *capable of adjustment*," and hoped I would
meet him alone, in an empty house, No. 1,
Berkeley-street, where he would wait for me. I
received this communication with doubt and
distrust. The measures adopted towards me, in
the effort to get rid of me, had been so strange,
that I was afraid to meet my husband " *alone, in
an empty house.*" But I agreed, on his petition,
to come to his own house. He then besought
me once more " to forget the past " and return
home. He laid the blame of all that had happened, on his friends and advisers; said the trial
was against his will and judgment, and that he
longed to " take me to his heart again." He
sent notes almost daily to my house. Those
letters began, " My Carry," " My dear Carry,"

and were signed, "Yours affectionately." Two
of them (in allusion to my fear of meeting him)
bore the playful signature of "GREENACRE,"—
the name of a man who had been recently hung,
for enticing a woman to his house by promising
marriage, and then murdering and cutting her
into pieces.

This planned reconciliation did not take place.
Mr Norton's sister informed him that I did not
intend "honestly" to return to him. That is
that I did not intend to *remain* in my home.
That I would go back for a triumph; for my
reputation and my children; but not to stay.
Renewed bitter disputes took place, and my
children were delivered over to his sister.

It cost Mr Norton nothing, to revert to the
hypocritical pretence he had adopted in the
action of damages. He, who had just written
those coaxing letters signed Greenacre,—who
had just begged his wife to "meet him in an
empty house," and try to arrange so as to out-
wit those who had been his "advisers,"—leaped
nimbly up again to the pedestal from which he
had descended, and resumed the attitude of an
"injured husband." Actually, the next step
after the GREENACRE letters, was to advertise me
in the English newspapers; Mr Norton being, I

believe, the only man of his own rank in life
who ever resorted to that measure.

When I saw this wonderful insult gazetted
by the husband who had just been wooing my
return:—" *Whereas on 30th March, 1830, my*
" *wife, Caroline Elizabeth Sarah, left me, her*
" *family, and home, and hath from thenceforth*
" *continued to live separate and apart from me,*"
&c.,—I again inquired if I had " no remedy? "
None. Only my brother's solicitors were directed
to publish a counter advertisement, declaring
the whole of what Mr Norton had stated was
false.

Afterwards, Sir John Bayley (Mr Norton's
own counsel) submitted his letters to Lord
Wynford (who had been Mr Norton's guardian).
Lord Wynford expressed himself in the strongest
and most contemptuous terms with respect to
his former ward; and finally—for the express
purpose of being shown to Mr Norton—he wrote
the following note (the original of which is in
my possession)—

 " *My Dear Bayley,*

  " *I have been thinking of the correspond-*
" *ence you read to me this morning. I am con-*
" *vinced that George Norton can have no defence*

" *to the actions, and that his defending them will* " *be attended* WITH LOSS OF CHARACTER, *as well* " *as great expense. He should agree to the ar-* " *rangement that you propose, or any other that* " *can be made. I will write to Grantley to tell* " *him that I have advised a settlement on* ANY " *terms.*"

" Faithfully yours,

" WYNFORD."

Mr Norton had given his pledged word in writing, to his counsel and referee, to abide by any decision he might come to. He broke his word, refused to abide by his written pledge, and actually had the effrontery to complain of his letters "having been shewn"! To which Sir John Bayley bluntly replied, that *if* he was doing what was right and honest by me, "it was astonishing he should so dread its being *known.*"

At length, after I had remained for two years without a farthing of support from my husband; dependent on my family; one of my creditors brought an action against Mr Norton; who once more undertook—(being the aggressor)—to pretend to be the aggrieved. Once more I, also, struggled to prove, under the blessed English law, what were the real facts of the case. My

husband himself has published, the reason of my
non-success. Here are Mr Norton's printed
words:—" *Lord Abinger, who tried the cause, upon*
" *a suggestion of my counsel*" *(Sir Fitzroy Kelly)*
" *that Sir John Bayley had been my advocate and*
" *referee,* REFUSED TO HEAR HIS EVIDENCE."
Lord Abinger refused the evidence which Lord
Wynford had warned Lord Grantley would be
fatal: the evidence of which Lord Wynford had
said, that *if* it should ever come out, it would be
attended " *with loss of character* " for Mr Norton.
It was suppressed: and because it was suppressed
the case was decided *for* Mr Norton instead of
against him, as Lord Wynford had warned him
must happen.

After this, Mr Norton proposed once more to
have " referees." He named Sir F. Thesiger,
whose opinion I give in his own words:—" *The*
" *accommodation proposed by Norton is one in*
" *which you are to give way upon every subject,*
" *and he is not to recede upon one ; and it seems*
" *to me to be ridiculous to talk of conciliation upon*
" *such a footing. . . . . . It is impossible not to be*
" *struck with the vacillating and vexatious course*
" *which Norton has pursued ; exciting hopes only*
" *to disappoint them, and making promises appa-*
" *rently for the opportunity of breaking them.*"

Why should there be no tribunal of control over these " vacillating" husbands, who refuse to abide by written pledges, and make promises " for the opportunity of breaking them"? Why is the absurd fiction of " non-existence', to be kept up *in law*, when *in fact*, two alienated parties exist, with adverse interests, struggling and antagonistic ?

One of the episodes of my " non-existence" in law, at this time, consisted in my having to endure a libel of immoderate length and bitterness, in the " British and Foreign Quarterly Review." I had made little struggle about other matters. I had yielded to Lord Melbourne's earnest request that, while he was minister, I would not publish my own account of the case between him and my husband. But resolutely, passionately, and till the final hour of success, I struggled against the law which enabled another woman to take *my children*. In the course of that struggle, I wrote two pamphlets: one, " On the Separation of Mother and Child;" the other, " A Plain Letter to the Chancellor, by Pierce Stevenson, Esq." The review in question attributed to me a paper I did *not* write, and never saw; " On the Grievances of Woman;" and boldly setting my name, in the index, as

the author, — proceeded, in language strange
rabid and virulent, to abuse the writer; calling
her a " SHE-DEVIL" and a " SHE-BEAST." No less
than one hundred and forty-two pages were devoted to the nominal task of opposing the Infant
Custody Bill, and in reality to abusing *me*.
Not being the author of the paper criticised,
I requested my solicitor to prosecute the Review
as a libel. He informed me that being a married
woman, I could not prosecute of myself; that
my husband must prosecute: my husband
—who had assailed me with every libel in his
power! There could be no prosecution: and I
was left to study the grotesque anomaly in law
of having my defence made *necessary*, — and
made *impossible*, — by the same person.

"Oh! but," — say those who have not studied
and suffered under the law, as I have, — " in
return for all this, the husband is responsible
for his wife's debts: that we all know!" Do
you? I will shew that not only he is not responsible for his wife's debts to others — but
he is not responsible for his own covenanted
debts to *her*. He is, as I have said, *legally*
responsible for nothing, but that she shall not
come upon the parish.

In 1848, my husband required ready money

to improve the estate left him by the woman to whom my children were at first taken.

In order to raise this money on the trust-funds of our marriage settlements, my signature was necessary. To obtain my signature, Mr. Norton drew up a contract. He dictated the terms of the contract himself; vehemently urged its completion; and reproached my solicitor for the delay, distrust, and reluctance, which I shewed before I signed it. I *did* eventually sign it; and so did Mr. Norton; and so, also, as I have already stated, did the Hon. Edmund Phipps (married to the widow of the Hon. Charles Norton, my husband's younger brother). The effect of my signature was, that Mr. Norton immediately raised the loan from our trust-fund, to employ on his estate. The effect of *his* signature, and the signatures of the Marquis of Normanby's brother, and the solicitor who drew it up, was absolutely *nil*.

In 1851, my mother died. She left me (through my brother, to guard it from my hus-band) a small annuity, as an addition to my income. Mr. Norton first endeavoured to claim her legacy, and then balanced the first payment under her will, by arbitrarily stopping my allow-ance. I insisted that the allowance was secured, by his own signature, and those other signatures, to a formal deed. He defied me to prove it,— " as, by law, man and wife were one, and could "not contract with each other; and the deed " was therefore good for nothing."

I confess I thought the fear of exposure would prevent his disputing the contract; I thought,— this time at least, the memorable words of Lord Wynford,—"*George Norton can have no defence to* " *the actions, and his defending them will be attended* " *with loss of character,*" must operate as a check upon so unfair, so monstrous an act, as availing himself of the legal fiction of my " non-existence," to escape from a written bond, which any one *not* his wife might have prosecuted upon.

I was mistaken. Not only Mr Norton held by the quibble that man and wife could not contract with each other; not only he did this,—but he had the base and cruel hypocrisy to once more drag forward Lord Melbourne's name, in order to make that seem *my* shame and *my* disgrace, which was in fact *his* shame and *his* disgrace; and to pretend wrong, where he knew he had been the wronger. Once more, for the sake of money,— as in the action for " damages,"—he endeavoured to cover me with opprobrium! Creeping back to his old place; scrambling up on the moss-covered and forsaken pedestal of "the injured husband"; he met the mother of his grown-up sons, with the accusations he had admitted to be a falsehood in their childhood : bruising those boyish hearts with forgotten slanders, first raised, and first *retracted*, when the eldest was but six years old!

He met me in person in the law court; he instructed his lawyer, in my very presence, what questions to ask me that could insult me most: and when that gentleman afterwards apologised for the tone of those questions, he asserted that Mr Norton's instructions went beyond what he had even ventured to ask!

He affected (O gross affectation!) to be hurt, as "an injured husband," at my accepting any assistance in money from Lord Melbourne's sister or family after his decease: and affirmed that he had made conditions with me about it. When I contradicted this on oath,—disproved it, and commented on the shameful pretence by which, in a dispute about my mother's will, he revived discussions about Lord Melbourne,— seeing that he himself retained one thousand a- year from Lord Melbourne's patronage,—(steadily preserving THAT memory of past favors, even through all the reviling of his dead patron),—

Mr Norton printed the wonderful falsehood, that
Lord Melbourne had given him the place he held,
"before he knew Mrs Norton!" The ridicule of
this—(even if true)—might have struck any
one; this new way of dividing the ledger; this
abhorrence of a man "because of the seduction
of my wife"—but satisfaction in the place obtained from him, because it was "*before* the
seduction of my wife." But I proved it *not* to
be true, by Lord Melbourne's own letters. It
was a sheer invention; and given with the most
careful detail. Yet Mr Norton,—convicted of
its being utterly false,—contented himself with
saying, "the matter had happened so long ago,"
he made an "unintentional mistake." How
many more of his false slanders against the dead
and the living are "unintentional mistakes"?

I will not pause over that question. I will
not pause over the still debateable point, whether
that signed paper, even if not a contract with *me*,
may not be held good as a contract with my
creditors;—a written and stamped agreement with
them, made by a magistrate and barrister; the
sole condition annexed being, that while it is
paid they shall not apply to him. Nor will I
enlarge further on the abuse and insult which
was showered on me that day in court, only for

G

asserting a just claim. INSULT is not DEGRADA-
TION: Queens have been insulted, as I was: and
the famous summons in Henry VIII.'s time—
"Katherine! come into court,"—was about as
just as that which called *me* there! It is enough
to know, that in this dispute between the existent
husband and the non-existent wife, the existent
husband had every advantage. The dead friend
and patron was scurrilously abused, by the man
who still holds place under his appointment.
The living but " non-existent" wife, was publicly
insulted, by the husband who had written her the
Greenacre letters, and entreated her return home
on the plea that she might "forgive" the trial,
since he disbelieved in its accusations! The
"existent" husband subpœnaed my bankers; compelled them to produce their books, and sent his
attorney to make extracts at their bank, of all
sums entered in my private account. He also
subpœnaed my publishers; to compel them to
declare what were the copyrights they held of
me, and what sums they had paid me: for,
(amazing to say,) the copyrights of my
works are *his*, by law: my very soul and brains
are not my own! And, when all was done, this
great *dictum* was impressed upon my memory;
that the contract was *nil*, because the fiction of

the law is, that "man and wife are one,"—and not two contracting parties; and Mr Norton, therefore, was not bound "in law," only "in honour."

I am not now discussing this, with any reference to him individually. Gone,—past—buried in unutterable scorn,—are the days in which I appealed, either *to* him or *from* him. I complain,—not of the existent husband, but of the existent law: and of that "nation of gallant gentlemen," who scarcely care, and scarcely know, what *is* the existing law on such subjects.

After the creditors' case was over, Mr Norton enquired, (the old enquiry!)—whether I would "submit to referees" the point, whether he ought "in honour" to abide by his signature; and whether I would name a referee on my part. I answered in the affirmative: and I named as my referee, one who may fairly claim to inspire as much confidence, respect, and universal esteem, from men of all ranks, ages, or parties, as I think it ever was the lot of any person to enjoy:—I named the Marquis of Lansdowne. Mr Norton proposed his own brother, Lord Grantley; which nomination was declined, as an impossible choice—*impossible*, recollecting the circumstances of the trial,—the residence of the witnesses, — and the nearness of connection. No other choice was proposed. Mr Norton either felt, (as he may truly feel), that no unprejudiced gentleman in England, would support him in his legal quibble:—or he had never intended to propose a choice which *could* be accepted,—which is more than probable.

———

Now I will pray your Majesty's attention to the effect of this non-existence in law, on the several parties involved in the discussion of this contract.

And first I will take Mr Norton's position.

From the date of my mother's death, he has withheld entirely, and with perfect impunity, my income as his wife. I do not receive, and have not received for the last three years, a single farthing from him. He retains, and always has retained, property that was left in my home—gifts made to me by my own family on my marriage, and to my mother by your Majesty's aunt, H.R.H. the Duchess of York;— articles bought from my literary earnings,— books which belonged to Lord Melbourne; and, in particular, a manuscript of which Lord Melbourne himself was the author, (when a very young man,) which Mr Norton resolutely refused to give up.

He receives from my trustees the interest of the portion bequeathed me by my father, who died in the public service, holding an official appointment at the Cape of Good Hope, leaving a family of very young orphans, slenderly provided for. If my father lived, it is to be presumed there is no man he would see with greater abhorrence than Mr Norton (considering what the fate of his daughter has been), yet such portion as he was able to leave me, goes from the "non-existent" wife, to the existent husband, in the general trust-fund of our marriage.

I have also (as Mr Norton impressed on me, by subpœnaing my publishers) the power of earning, by literature,—which fund (though it be the grant of Heaven, and not the legacy of earth) is no more legally mine than my family property.

Now again, I say, is or is not this a ridiculous law (if laws be made to conduct to justice)? I cannot divorce my husband, either for adultery, desertion, or cruelty; I *must* remain married to *his name; he* has, in right of that fact (of my

link to his name), a right to everything I have
in the world—and I have no more claim upon
him, than any one of your Majesty's ladies in
waiting, who are utter strangers to him! I
never see him:—I hear of him only by attacks
on my reputation:—and I do not receive a
farthing of support from him. His reply, by
attorney (dated 10th of April, this session), to
any such demand—is to bid the creditor "examine the will of my mother in Doctors' Commons" (thereby throwing off the mask of pretence he wore, and standing openly on his legal
irresponsibility): and when we first separated,
he offered me, as sole provision, a small pension
paid by Government to each of my father's children; reckoning that pension as *his!*

———

That is the position of the husband.

The next startling point, is the position of the
trades-people under this " non-existent" rule ;
and if the opinion of persons so humble were
likely to reach your Majesty, they could tell you
what *they* think of the law which leaves *them*
utterly without any remedy.

In the creditor's action tried on Mr Norton's

contract, the plaintiff was Mr Thrupp, one of the coachmakers " by appointment " to your Majesty. Mr Thrupp lost his cause as against Mr Norton; and perhaps the uninitiated imagine it was merely a question which of us should pay him ; or pay any other creditor. Those who think so, are mistaken. In consequence of this rule of my " non-existence," Mr Thrupp, and the group of creditors, can claim payment from *no one*. They cannot sue the " non-existent " married woman ; the husband cannot *contract* with the "non-existent" married woman; and the "non-existent" married woman cannot be compelled to pay, if she refuses to discharge the debt. " Oh! but you will *not* refuse; you will pay, surely," say the bystanders. How? My husband owes me £1,500, or three years' income. I have no means of raising this large sum; no one would lend money to a married woman; she can give no security. Besides, I am in debt to my bankers: obstinately disbelieving in the possibility of the law's injustice (before it was proved to me), I borrowed from *them*, when Mr Norton stopped my allowance : and that loan, with interest, is still unpaid. I am in debt to my printers; for work arising out of this very injustice. I have persons who receive regular instalments every year, on past dues; I have other employment for my money, than making up Mr Norton's defalcations.

"Oh! but you should not have other employment: you should write and earn money, and pay these people; and then economize, and re-trench, so as to give up the £500 a year to Mr Norton."

Why?

Why, because I am married to a name,—am I to strive and labour, to enable the owner of that name to commit a direct fraud? Why am *I* to pay Mr Norton's debts, to renounce all claim on him, and admit that my legal "non-existence" made our signing that contract a mere farce? simply because he has grossly and cruelly insulted and slandered me, in an open court of justice, on grounds he *knew* were false; and with a defence absolutely fictitious?

I would not if I could! If all England were to agree to raise a shilling subscription,—or if some one were to do what Mr Kennedy of the Woods and Forests says has been done for him, —namely, come forward and say, " I think this " business so unjust, that *I* will settle for life the "income you lose; now pay your people,"—I would not admit that the matter should end so!

I do not consider this as MY cause: though it is
a cause of which (unfortunately for me) I am
an illustration. It is the cause of *all* the women, and of a large proportion of the trades-
people, in England. If I were personally set at
ease about it to-morrow, that would not alter
the *law*. The same injustice might happen next
day to some woman who could not struggle, or
earn, or write; for whom no one would come
forward; and to some petty tradesman,—not
like Mr Thrupp, coachmaker to your Majesty,
in a large way of business,—but grievously
injured by the loss of even a small sum. What
is needed, is not the arranging of one particular
case, but a Tribunal of Control, a Tribunal for
Marriage and Divorce; to decide ALL such cases;
—and to prevent the possibility of the shame to
England and to English law, entailed by throwing the sum secured by a magistrate's signature,
the signatures of two peers' brothers, and a lawyer,—among a tradesman's list of "bad debts."

The tradesman is cheated;—not by me, for I
am cheated in my turn; nor (except indirectly)
by Mr Norton, for it is his wife whom *he* defrauds. It is the LAW that cheats the tradesman. The law,—that should do him justice!
He loses justice; he loses the sum due as the

actual debt; and he loses the expenses of applying for that debt unsuccessfully. Is that, or is
it not, a ridiculous confusion of laws, to exist in
any kingdom?

I will take, now, your Majesty's position; for,
—be it said with all respect and loyalty,—this
was no common "private quarrel," of which
scarce an echo can reach the throne: but a
matter which it would be wanting in reverence
to believe, *can* have been indifferent to you. The
first Prime Minister of your Majesty's reign is
scurrilously attacked and slandered in the English newspapers, by an English magistrate. In
a long letter published by that magistrate (expressly, as he informs his readers, in his "public
capacity"), he accuses the dead minister, who
cannot defend himself, not only of the seduction
of his wife, but of bribery, malversation, cor-
ruption, and baseness of every kind.

The magistrate who makes these accusations,
has been stigmatised by each successive person,
called (even by himself) to interfere in our
quarrel, as entirely regardless of TRUTH. The
clergyman of Westminster Chapel, immediately

after our parting, wrote to me, of Mr Norton's
"amazing assertions," and his attempt to obtain
a retractation of their falsehood. Lord Melbourne gave his word of honour that the accusation on which the action for damages was
based, was false; and he believed it was brought
for money. My brother (through his solicitor)
declared every word of my husband's advertisement against me in the papers in 1839 to be
false. Lord Wynford in 1838 declared the dis-
crepancy to be so great between Mr Norton's
real case, and his pretence of being an offended
husband, that the public knowledge of it must
be attended "with loss of character." Mr
Norton's own counsel, Sir John Bayley, published, in 1853, this declaration; "nearly every
"statement he made me, turned out to be *untrue*."
Sir F. Thesiger said his promises seemed made
"apparently for the opportunity of breaking
"them." ALL accused him of untruth; at all
times; down to that unpardonable (and un-
pardoned) day of August, 1853, when he met
me in a law court with a fictitious plea of slander,
and was contradicted *on oath* by the witnesses:
to that 24th August, when his letter of explanation was disproved by me, and his false account
of his appointment by Lord Melbourne publicly

exposed: to that 31st of August, when the solicitor who drew up the contract declared of his
statement with reference to that matter—" the
" entire paragraph is untrue;" to that memorable
13th of September, 1853, when Sir John Bayley
finally contradicted, point by point, every invention and slanderous assertion he had put forward.
That such a man,—*proved* to be so recklessly
false,—should have any power at all over the
reputation of the dead or the living, arises out
of the law which permits an "action for damages,"
as a sort of gambling speculation, without defence or contradiction being possible to the wife;
and the law which allows the breach of contract
on plea of " non-existence " of the wife; for it
is on these two links of opportunity that Mr
Norton has connected the long chain of false-
hoods against Lord Melbourne and myself.

I think it is in the Duc de St. Simon's Me-
moirs, that a passage occurs, which her Majesty,
the Queen of Holland, first pointed out to me;
where, speaking of the death of one dear to the
throne, the author says that the king lamented,
—" *mais un peu à la Royale,*"—implying (as
many historical and even Scriptural phrases
imply), that the friends of kings and princes are
sooner forgotten, and less grieved for, than friends

of equal degree. Certainly there can be no entire friendship, where there is no real equality; but there may be memory of service and an earnest regard; and I will not believe (for *he* would not have believed it) that the abuse of Lord Melbourne was indifferent to your Majesty. Leaning on the hand of that loyal and true friend and servant, your Majesty ascended the throne of your ancestors; and the Queen of three kingdoms said to her minister, " Help me,"—as she placed her foot on the steps. Soon after your Majesty's accession, he read to you (in that magnificent and melodious voice which many still remember), those verses from the Third Book of Kings, where the youthful Solomon, being asked by God in a dream, what gift he will desire at the beginning of his inexperienced reign; asks, not "*long life, nor riches, nor the lives of his* "*enemies,*" — but " *an understanding heart; to* "*judge the people, and discern between good and* " *evil.*" Lord Melbourne held *then*, a position which has scarcely a parallel in English history; —the extreme youth and sex of his Sovereign, mingling with his duties as counsellor something of the character of a guardian. That he fulfilled those anxious duties, while he lived, with devoted zeal, and was worthy to fulfil them, no one has ever doubted.

When, after his death, rumours and aspersions respecting the interference of Prince Albert with public affairs, found their way from conversational gossip into print, and were made a subject of discussion by various organs of the press, Lord Aberdeen in the House of Lords, and Lord John Russell in the Commons, read aloud, to eager and attentive members, a brief frank note, written by Lord Melbourne to your Majesty, expressive of his favorable opinion of the discretion, - ability, and excellence of the Prince Consort. And this minister was so trusted for wisdom and for honesty, was held to be such an authority in matters of the deepest moment to England's welfare, that those few lines were received with a burst of cordial cheering, such as many a long and eloquent oration has failed to produce.

He will read, counsel, instruct, and serve no more. Nor is it in human nature that his memory among those who knew him should not fade. But I will not believe that he was lamented so much " *à la Royale*,"—that he held so brief a lease in his Sovereign's regard, — that even

while his letter was quoted, he himself was forgotten!

For *his* sake,—if not for the great sake of
justice, which all rulers must reverence,—I feel
a deep conviction it was far otherwise with your
Majesty; and that when you found one of the
magistrates of your City of London (a magistrate by Lord Melbourne's own appointment)
suddenly filling the principal journals of that
city with base, false, and rancorous abuse of
your Majesty's dead friend and servant, it was
painful—*not* indifferent—to the Royal mind.

What then? Why *this:* that the throne was
then mocked—as justice was mocked—as the
decency of social order was mocked,—by this
impunity of atrocious libel on a minister whose
character stood so admittedly high, that even
one of his posthumous notes was deemed of
sufficient authority to define the position, and to
declare the character, of the Consort of the
Sovereign! And this impunity of abuse,—by
this minister's own nominee, — not even the
Queen of England could prevent or punish,
because there exists in her realm no legal tribunal which could have taken cognisance of this
quarrel *from the first*,—and have ended its disputes, and silenced its ever-recurring scandal,

seventeen years ago, by a timely decision between the irresponsible husband and the " non-existent" wife.

———

As to my own position,—if others were as weary of reading, as I am of writing, the subject must indeed be tedious: but it is necessary to my summing up. I am, as regards my husband, in a worse position than if I had been divorced. In that case, Englishmen are so generous, that some chivalrous-hearted man might perhaps have married and trusted me, in spite of the unjust cloud on my name. I am *not* divorced, and I cannot divorce my husband; yet I can establish no legal claim upon him, nor upon any living human being! My reputation, my property, my happiness, are irrevocably in the power of this slanderer on false grounds; this rapacious defender of his right to evade written bonds. I cannot release myself. I exist and I suffer; but the law denies my existence.

I have two sons. One already launched in life, employed in your Majesty's service among junior diplomates: and one who is not yet in any profession.

He is not in any profession, because at the
very moment when I had promised and arranged
so to dispose of him, Mr Norton made it *impossible*, by breaking the contract which secured my
allowance; and took away my means of doing so.

Mr Norton stands on the legal ground, that
not only my mother's will (which he desires my
tradesmen to "inspect at Doctors' Commons"),
and other resources, would release him from the
necessity of supporting me,—but that I am so
able with my pen, I might *earn* £500 a year if
I worked hard enough! Would the Duke of
Bedford and Lord Westminster (two, I believe,
of your Majesty's wealthiest subjects) accept
from Mr Norton, instead of money due to them,
the assurance that he considered them quite
sufficiently well off without it? And if it were
true that my literary earnings could be perma-
nent and constant, on what conceivable principle
of justice am I to toil, in order to hand over my
allowance as Mr Norton's wife, to be spent on
his mistress or divided amongst several mistresses,—instead of preventing my younger son
from wasting his talents and energies without a
career; or affording further assistance to the
eldest—the wisest, kindest, and best son who

H

ever struggled to do difficult duty between the parents of a divided home?

I owe to the law which enables Mr Norton to evade his contract, two lost years in my younger son's life,—(at the very moment of youth when employment is of most paramount importance); together with the breach of all my written engagements in his behalf. Mischievous and absurd, not only with reference to *me*, but to those dearest to me, is this quibble of "nonexistence" by which all my natural rights revert to the husband,—on whom I have no claim,—and who yet draws portions of his income from the dead man he publicly libels as my lover, and the dead father, whose daughter he seeks publicly to brand as a wanton!

The natural position of woman is inferiority to man. Amen! That is a thing of God's appointing, not of man's devising. I believe it sincerely, as a part of my religion : and I accept it as a matter proved to my reason. I never pretended to the wild and ridiculous doctrine of equality. I will even hold that (as one coming under the general rule that the wife must be inferior to the husband), *I* occupy that position. *Uxor fulget radiis Mariti;* I am Mr Norton's inferior; I am the clouded moon of that sun.

Put me then—(my ambition extends no further)
—in the same position as all his other inferiors!
In that of his housekeeper, whom he could not
libel with impunity, and without possible defence; of an apprentice whom he could not
maltreat lawlessly, even if the boy "condoned"
original ill-usage; of a scullion, whose wages he
could not refuse on the plea that she is legally
"non-existent"; of the day-labourer, with whom
he would not argue that his signature to a contract is "worthless." Put me under *some* law
of protection; and do not leave me to the mercy
of one who has never shewn me mercy. For
want of such a law of protection, all other protection has been vain! I have had the uphold-
ing (and I set it first, because it has been of
greater comfort and value to me than any other),
of as generous and affectionate a family as ever
combined to shield one of its members from
undeserved disgrace. Sisters. of spotless reputation, who stood by me "through evil report
and good report," tenderly and steadily for
restless years. Brothers and brothers-in-law,
among the best gentlemen of England. Relations and intimate friendships among the noblest
and purest of its women.

I have sons whom I love and am proud of,

and who (thank God!), love and are proud of *me*, in spite of past misery. I had the verdict of twelve English gentlemen, sworn to a verdict of *truth;* and the solemn word,—living and dying,—of the friend who was accused with me of sin. I was aided in my first battle against fortune, by persons of great rank and influence. By none more kindly than by your Majesty's uncle, the King of the Belgians: he who learned, perhaps, to feel more, having suffered more, than others; and who remembered me in my early girlhood, and in my mother's home: he who once held in England the place Prince Albert now fills: who was husband and father to the heirs of the English crown; and who, in the prime and pride of his own youth, saw the sun set one December night on that triumphantly happy position, and saw it rise—a childless widower!

I have had sympathy and assistance from obscurer friends; not noble in name, though noble in nature: and I have had with me, public opinion, and the good wishes of good hearts To what end? Vain, though not valueless, has been this accumulation of kindness, from friends, relatives and strangers, for want of such laws of protection! They could *pity*,—but they could not *help*. They could prevent nothing that has been inflicted on me: redress nothing: uor blot anything out.

————

In the course of my life, I have seen but one more resolute attempt at annulling the effect of the law on a woman's destiny; and I conceive even that to have failed. It was tried under the most favourable circumstances. Not, as in my case, in the reign of a Queen,—where, though no Salique law rules the succession, the general spirit of the laws and of opinion is against the importance of women: a Queen married to a foreign Prince, of less rank than the former Queen's consorts in England,—prudently and unremittingly occupied, ever since he reached our shores, in conciliating the Tory party; among whom (and especially among those employed at Court), stood Lord Melbourne's bitterest foes. Not under these disadvantages, but in the strong reign of a King:—with our modern Marl-borough,—our one General,—the late Duke of Wellington,—for the lady's unflinching friend,—the experiment of support was tried, and failed. A pension of £380 a year on the Irish Civil List was granted to the maligned wife. She was afterwards made extra Lady in Waiting to Queen Adelaide: and all that great friends, great influence, and court favour could do for her, was done; the husband vainly attacking the Duke of Wellington, in a published pamphlet, for his interference in his domestic affairs; and vainly deprecating what was done, as done in defiance of himself, the lord and ruler of that broken home.

But set that woman's destiny to rights, the Court could *not:* nor break her marriage: nor overrule what was determined by her husband as to her more intimate destiny, — the dear tie of children, or attacks on her reputation. The throne could *compensate*, but not *redress:* could compensate in this one instance, but could not prevent such instances from recurring: could give that woman her place among court pageants, but could not prevent her heart aching beneath her diamonds: nor create, by any number of royal smiles, a recurring dawn for that light, which, when a woman's home-destiny is wrecked, goes out into utter darkness.

It is a glorious thing that the Law should be stronger than the Throne. It is one of dear boastful England's proudest blind boasts. But

it is *not* a glorious thing that, being stronger
than the throne, it should be weaker than the
subject: and that that which even a king can
only do within a certain limit,—(oppress or uphold),—may be done with boundless irresponsible power, in the one single relation of husband
and wife.

———

I have seen,—*per contrâ,*—*one* instance of an
English gentleman crushed, denounced, and so-
cially disgraced, as well as legally condemned.
It was for an accusation of unfair play at cards.
A morbid desire to win,—without even the motive of the needy sharper—poverty,—upset the
calculations of his playmates, and rendered their
game of skill a game of chance. Oh! what a
turmoil this discovery created! Nothing else
was thought of: the still pond of polite society,
with its quiet surface of duck-weed and ornamental lilies, turned suddenly into a foaming
whirlpool: the lilies were tossed like sea-weed
in a storm. The idea of WHIST-PLAYING being
disturbed; the pleasures of club-loungers in-
fringed upon by such dreadful uncertainties;
the good old-fashioned games that wiled away

their unoccupied evenings, turned into traps
for their purses—the sacred cards scored with
private methods of identification — this indeed
was an outrage on social life, law, and order!
This could not,—would not,—must not be borne
for one day after it became known! Accordingly,
the most vigorous measures were taken—law
proceedings were instituted: everybody was
shocked beyond measure: examinations were
gone through: old companions were summoned
to give evidence against him, and gave it; some
with tears in their eyes and some without. The
thunder of public reprobation rolled round his
head; the lightning of a legal condemnation
reached and struck him; and, when the storm
was over,— when the calm of polite life was
restored,—when the lilies and the slack duck-
weed settled down once more on the surface of
their much disturbed pond, its waters had closed
for ever over the wrecked destiny of that popular
and accomplished man!

———

Since then, I have seen every species of cheating, unfairness, tyranny and oppression, as regards *women*, borne with the most comfortable

indifference. The lilies and the duckweed lie
smiling and sleeping; and they think it vulgar,
and very troublesome, if wrongs that do not
wrong their pleasures, and struggles to amend
laws that are already quite perfect enough to
protect those pleasures,—are forced on their un-
willing notice! Let whist-playing, not women,
be protected: the one signifies, the other don't.
The club-loungers smile in scorn. " What is
" all this disturbance about? Woman's rights
" and woman's wrongs?—pooh, pooh; nonsense;
" Bloomerism; Americanism! we can't have that
" sort of thing in England. Women must sub-
" mit; those who don't, are bad women—depend
" upon it: all bad women. There are no bad
" men. Who ever heard of a bad man? or, at
" least, of his conduct being condemned by the
" world at large, in matters like these?" " But
" this really *is* a monstrous case." " Well, yes,
" it's all very wrong—very shabby—very un-
" principled—certainly; but we can't meddle;
" *all* the laws respecting women are in a hope-
" less state of confusion; and it is much better
" one or two women should suffer unjustly, than
" that the authority of husbands should be
" doubted. As to a husband's sin, and all that,
" it *can't* signify so much as the woman's sin;

" because, you know the woman's sin may give
" her husband a spurious child to inherit his
" property."

Now where is the logic of this reasoning?
Why is it better one or two (or one or two hundred) women should suffer? It is not better
that one or two apprentices should be starved or
maltreated, rather than interfere with the authority of their masters; nor one or two factory
children, rather than interfere with manufac-
turers: women are not appealing *for an exceptional law in their favour;* on the contrary, they
are appealing not to be made an exception from
the general protection of the laws. As to the
comparative harmlessness of the husband's sin,
what does that mean? It means merely that *in
his own home* his sin has no result; but in the
other home, where he sins? How do you
guarantee that his sin shall harm no one? Why
is he to have the liberty to wrong others,—by a
wrong that in his own case would be so intolerable and unpardonable,—when the same reasoning may be applied to the wrong he does, as to
the wrong he suffers? May not *he,* also, be the
father of a spurious child?—one born in a
friend's home?—one born, perhaps, of some
poor victim tempted to cast it into that cold

grey river, which runs past the Senate-house where these hard laws are so falsely argued, and past the Temple where they are so carelessly studied!

This is the same England where such an outcry was raised against General Haynau, that he was afterwards assaulted in the public streets! Austrians might well retort upon Englishmen the faultfinding in which they then indulged. There is not one of that aristocracy of gentlemen, who would not smile in scorn at the Englishman's affectation of a better law for women in his own country. Is there no pain and degradation except *physical* pain and degradation? Is there no indecency but in ideas of nudity?— no barbarity but in stripes and blows? Is there no brutality in the cross-examination in divorce cases, from which even the female servants shrink, angry and wounded, at being so questioned? Is there no indecency in the trials before the House of Lords, which Lord Beaumont termed " disgusting and demoralizing ?" Is there no pain in the hunting down for feverish years, with torment and libel, a woman who can escape from neither?

And yet these English hearts are noble. From among these " club-loungers" we have sent the

bravest men that ever perished patiently, or with
glorious courage, on a disastrous battle-field.
Among them there is not one who would not
guard the woman of his own family from insult
with his life; with as much chivalry as those
knights of romance who in less civilized days
fought a hand-to-hand battle, for the fame or
the rights of the weaker sex. Only they cannot be brought to believe that *they* can interfere
in a revision of the law, or to consider the necessity of such revision. They love and revere
particular names among women. Their hearts
glow at the devotion of the poor girl Grace
Darling, whose impulsive heroism saved wrecked
sailor's lives: at the gentle prison-visitings of
Mrs Fry: at the Crimean pilgrimage of mercy
and sick tendance, undertaken by Miss Nightingale and her companions. They were all for
erecting a " Monument to Grace Darling;" the
newspapers at the time were filled with such
schemes.

But when Miss Nightingale (please God!)
shall return safe amongst us: when she shall
cease from gazing in the great multitude of wist-
ful dying eyes, and come back to the usual sights
of life: when the moans of the wounded shall be
a sorrowful memory, not a painful reality in her

ears: when, instead, she shall hear, as she lands on her native soil, the shouted welcomes of applauding and reverential hearts, —will it ever occur to the men of England that the best " testi-" monial" to the worth of such women, would be to give the sex they belong to, a status, which, in our country alone, is denied them? and laws of protection, which France, Germany, Prussia, —aye, even Austria and Russia,—find it easier to enact than ourselves.

It will go hard with the loyalty of such of your Majesty's female subjects as suffer like me, but they will wish themselves subjects in any other country; where, at least, if they *are* to suffer, they must offend against the law, and not, as in England, suffer without offending. The Haynaus of England are they who will not help to change such laws! Had I been a man, I would have worked out their revision and reform: but I am only a woman—and, in the land which my Queen governs, women count for nothing in important matters. I am only a woman—and by the law taught in those Inns of Court where the Prince Consort is a Bencher, my existence is " absorbed in that of my hus-" band;" and my intelligence is only so far available, that it enables him to subpœna my publishers into Court, to prove that I can earn my bread without compelling him to support me.

Even now, friends say to me:—" Why write? "why struggle? it is the law! You will do no "good." But if every one slacked courage with that doubt, nothing would ever be achieved in this world. This much I will do,—woman though I be. I will put on record,—in French, German, English, and Italian,—what the law for women was in England, in the year of civilization and Christianity 1855, and the 16th year of the reign of a female sovereign! *This*, I will do; and others who come after me may do more. My son, or my grandson, may be Lord Chancellor of England, and may do with this abuse of justice, what Romilly and Erskine (the latter of my mother's race) did with abuses of justice in their day; and what Brougham and Lyndhurst have done with abuses of justice in ours. The feudal barbarity of the laws between " Baron and Feme " may vanish from amongst us, as the feudal barbarity of duelling has vanished; which is already a checked abuse, and a forgotten fashion.

My son, I say, or my grandson, may achieve this reform; and my memory may be with them while they work, helpless as I am now! Is this

a dream to smile at ? This is not a day to smile
at *any* boast of what accidental circumstance or
individual energy may bring about We have
lately seen examples of changed fortune, wild
as the dreams of Alnaschar, but more suc-
cessful.

Sixty-eight years ago, on the deck of a vessel
struggling through a stormy passage to the
island of Martinique, sate the mournful mother
of a little girl only three years old. This mother
was young, beautiful, forsaken. Her husband,
being weary of her, had become "a little profli-
"gate,"—and the wife, yearning,—as many a
broken-hearted girl has yearned before, under
such circumstances of neglect and disappoint-
ment, for the old dear home of her childhood,—
was returning to her parents and friends. There
was no fierceness in that woman's heart. Her
grief was the gentle grief of Faust's Margaret:—

„Ich wein',—ich wein',—ich weine!"

In love, and generous devotion through life, she
had scarcely her equal; and she had through
life the fate those women who seem to deserve it
least, oftenest obtain For that mournful Creole,
weeping alone on the stormy seas,—helplessly

returning to her own family,—was Josephine de
Beauharnais, the neglected wife of the Vicomte
de Beauharnais, afterwards the repudiated Empress of Napoleon I., and that little child—who
sate trembling in the storm by its mother's side,
—was Hortense, afterwards Queen of Holland,
and mother of Napoleon III.

If,—as that Creole mother wept,—some voice
had whispered,—" Your lot is grief; grief now,
" and grief, in spite of splendour, in the years
" to come: but you shall be Empress of France:
" the little girl by your side shall be a Queen;
" her son an Emperor; and the music of a
" chance love-song which that child shall com-
" pose in after years, shall become the great
" solemn march and national hymn of France;
" for ever making melody of triumph in her
" son's ears, whether sounding on his native
" shores among millions of electing subjects, or
" played in the royal palaces of a rival nation,
" proud of reckoning on his friendship and
" alliance; proud of hearing that melody become
" a familiar companion to their own 'God save
" the Queen!' "—I say, if such a whisper had
come on the wild wind, and mingled with the
dash of the stormy spray, would not the fervent-
hearted Creole have shuddered with fear, lest

delirium—not hope—had taken possession of her mind?

Exactly forty years before this present time, Napoleon the First, conquered by the allies, came on board the English ship of war, the "Bellerophon." He proposed himself as a guest; and had to surrender as a prisoner. He asked permission to reside an exile in England, and was ordered under closest guard to St. Helena. The officers of his suite had their arms taken from them. The Emperor himself was refused any title but that of General Bonaparte, as "Head of the Army;" though he scornfully remarked that they might as well call him an archbishop, for he had also been "Head of the Church," and that at least he should be First Consul, England having sent ambassadors to him by that style and title. He wrote a vain appeal to the Prince Regent—"le plus puissant, "le plus constant, le plus genereux de mes "ennemis;" he entered a vain protest against being sent to his island prison. He said he never would go there; he refused to nominate the persons who were to accompany him. He wrote to the English ministry,—"Je ne suis "point prisonnier; je suis l'hôte de l'Angleterre." "La foi Britannique se trouvera perdue dans

I

" l'hospitalité du Bellerophon." But the proud
heart had to yield. His generals were deprived
of their arms. Bonaparte alone was "*permitted*"
to wear his sword when quitting the ship, by
special order from Admiral Lord Keith.

When transferred from the Bellerophon to
the Northumberland, his baggage was examined;
and from the boxes containing money, his valet
was permitted to take out such sum as was considered necessary for paying the wages of servants who were to be left behind, for *all* were
not allowed to accompany him. One box (containing four thousand gold Napoleons) was
detained; though afterwards delivered to Sir
Hudson Lowe to be returned to its owner. That
these proceedings were unexpected, and inex-
plicable to the French, we may presume from
the impossibility of persuading the two generals,
Savary and Lallemand, that the next step would
not be to deliver them up for execution to the
French Government; and by the attempt made
by the wife of General Bertrand to drown herself from the cabin window of the English ship,
as soon as the decision of the Prince Regent
became known.

If any prophet had then said to that baffled
man and conquered hero, Napoleon the First:—

" You cannot escape: Fate has overtaken you:
" humiliation, exile, sickness, and death, are now
" your only possible portion: nor shall even your
" son by your Austrian bride succeed you,—
" though you wedded to found a dynasty on the
" hope of his birth! But the grandson of your
" abjured and repudiated Josephine, shall, after
" many vicissitudes, obtain peaceable possession
" of the throne of France; and shall be the chief
" ally and friend of your enemy England. By
" a strange concurrence of accidents, the nephew
" of your conqueror the Duke of Wellington,
" shall be the English Ambassador to your
" nephew's Court at Paris. When your nephew
" goes (as he *will* go) on a triumphal visit to
" Great Britain, the English people shall throng
" and crowd and swarm round the statue of the
" Duke of Wellington (cast from the iron of his
" victories, and in memory of Waterloo), and
" climb up the railing round its pedestal, to
" see your namesake go by, and cheer him as he
" passes. And when, with the fair Consort who
" shall be his Empress, he visits in state the
" Italian Opera House in England; the beautiful
" Duchess of Wellington,—wife of your con-
" queror's son,—and her cousin, the Marchioness
" of Ely, shall be the attendant ladies, *standing*

I 2

" in graceful ceremony, while the Third Napoleon
" and his Eugenie, shall be seated in friendly
" equality of discourse with Victoria, Queen of
" Great Britain; the niece and successor of that
" Prince Regent to whom your vain appeal was
" written; by whom the irrevocable decree of
" your exile and nothingness was pronounced.

" Nor shall the sum of French gold detained
" on board the Bellerophon, be a near equivalent
" for the aggregate sums spent in preparation
" and feasting, in sight-seeings and rejoicings, by
" that changed England which desires worthily
" to receive your imperial successor. The City
" of London shall bid him to a festival where all
" things shall be memories of the past. The
" porcelain on which the meats are served, shall
" be painted for the occasion with *your* arms;
" the doyleys shall be green velvet and gold
" spangled with your imperial bees. The wines
" shall include, Malvoisie grown on Mount Ida,
" where Jupiter was nursed, — and Amontillado
" 'supplied at £600 a butt to Napoleon I.'
" And that Guildhall, whose Mayor, Aldermen,
" and Common Council once addressed Alexander
" of Russia in congratulations on your downfall,
" which they termed, ' *the deliverance of the*
" ' *afflicted nations of Europe from the most galling*

" ' *oppression and unprecedented tyranny that ever*
" ' *visited the human race*,' — shall echo equally
" flattering addresses to your nephew, united
" with the English *against* Russia, and yearning
" for the downfall of Alexander's heir. And
" whereas two grievous orders have fretted your
" officers; viz.: that all arms of every descrip-
" tion are to be taken from Frenchmen of all
" ranks on board this ship, and that only twelve
" domestics shall be permitted to attend the
" Emperor and suite to St. Helena, (by which
" many of them must go without their servants),
" —your nephew shall send, with his horses
" alone, sixteen grooms to the royal stables; and
" under triumphal arches, and palace portals,
" the English soldiers shall present arms to him
" as he passes : while, patiently awaiting his
" arrival in the great fortified port of Dover, he
" shall find the Prince Consort of England,
" Prince Albert of Saxe Cobourg; nephew of
" Leopold of Saxe Cobourg, who wedded your
" enemy the Prince Regent's only child—and
" wedded, after her death, the King of France's
" daughter; in the vacated throne of which last
" king, your nephew shall hold regal state, such
" as no former Monarch of France has ever
" surpassed."

I say, if—in his mournful passage to St.
Helena,—or in his lone, sad, angry rides, to and
from Longwood,—or in dreary days, when gazing
across the surrounding waste of sea that divided
him from the triumph of battles, and a throned
destiny, and the endearments of wife and son, and
consigned him to a living death, — this startling
sketch of the future has been suggested as possible,
by Montholon, or Bertrand, or Las Casas, when
talking with their imperial master, would not'
even Napoleon have deemed it a vain dream?

Or (more marvellous yet) if, at a date not
known to us, because too obscure, when Mr
Kirkpatrick, a Scotch gentleman, was doing duty
as consul at Malaga; worried with the petty details of his consulate position; the clash of mercantile interests, the perplexities of international
law, the claims of mariners, the jealousies of
residents, the broiling heat of the southern
climate, and the disputes about nothing, which
are always, in all consulates, arising about twice
every month, and are always said in the most
imminent degree to threaten " the dignity of the
" British flag,"—if, at that time, Mr Kirkpatrick,
leaning back in his chair, had said, " This is all
" very annoying, certainly; but I bear it with
" the more cheerfulness, as one result of my

" residing in this Spanish town will be, that my
" daughter shall marry a Spanish grandee; and
" the daughter of that marriage, being gifted
" with great beauty and grace, shall, all in good
" time, go to England as visitor on equal terms
" with England's Queen. Workmen shall hammer,
" and hang, and gild, day and night, to prepare a
" sleeping apartment, and sitting apartment,
" in Windsor Castle, worthy to receive her; and
" the Queen shall stand on her own threshold,
" to give her welcome and guide her in. A
" young and beautiful English marchioness shall
" be specially appointed to wait upon her. She
" shall be ushered hither and thither by the
" Prince Consort of Great Britain. Balls shall
" be given at court, at which she shall reign
" undisputed star; the one lovely sight, of which
" all eyes endeavour to catch a glimpse, be it ever
" so fleeting. And all this shall be done for my
" dear grand-daughter, in right of her marriage
" with the grandson of another gentleman, of no
" greater rank than myself; an advocate and
" judge at Ajaccio in Corsica; because that gen-
" tleman's son, a young artillery officer of great
" military genius, became so powerful and so
" famous, that he was crowned Emperor of
" France; made his brothers kings; his sisters

" queens ; and grew, indeed, so formidable to
" Europe, that England, Russia, Austria, and
" Prussia, combined to annihilate his power; and
" secured him at length as the prisoner of that
" very England—where the consul of Malaga's
" grand-daughter shall, as I tell you, have so
" brilliant a reception, in right of her marriage
" with the advocate of Ajaccio's grandson"!

If Mr Kirkpatrick had held this language,
and had made this Cassandra-like prophecy, while
these events were as yet not even "looming in
the distance," would not such persons as were
interested in his welfare, have written home to
his friends, to tell them that " poor Mr. Kirkpatrick was gone out of his mind;"—and the
next eager candidate for the Malaga consulship,
have privately put his friends on the alert as to
applications to government on his behalf,—" as it
" was probable there would be an immediate
" vacancy, on account of the melancholy visita-
" tion with which it had pleased Heaven to
" afflict the present consul"?

God only sets the measure of *what may be :*
and I say my son or grandson may be Lord
Chancellor, and may alter these laws in favour
of the lawless, at present in force in England.
We have seen the last member of the marvellous

Corsican family, whose history I have been sketching — (the present ruler of France) — declare to his Senate, that he fears assassination the less, because he believes he has a mission from Heaven yet unaccomplished. *I* believe,—in my obscurer position,—that I am permitted to be the example on which a particular law shall be reformed. Does that also create a smile? It is, nevertheless, only one form of belief in a special Providence. If that is a ridiculous belief, what becomes of our " days of humiliation,"—" special prayers,"—" fasts of propitiation,"—and perpetual calls upon Heaven to interfere in the affairs of man? If it be a rational, and *not* a ridiculous belief, where does the interposition of Heaven begin and end? Does Providence only condescend to look down on people and objects that we poor worms, (in this speck of one of His million worlds,) choose to consider "important"? Does it only interfere in behalf of sovereigns, nations, and aggregate interests? Must the notice of Heaven be first attracted by the distinctions of earth? Must the proper objects for selection be marked by blue ribands, made out of the cocoons God gave as a covering for a moth's unfinished wings,—ore and precious stones, which He scattered in the

clay we tread upon,—and tossing plumes, which
were once the tail and wing feathers of a desert
bird, fleeing before man over the hot sands,
part of whose track man shall never see: part
of whose track, till the day when earth consumes
away like a scroll, shall remain among God's
"waste and barren places"; glowing in arid and
insufferable loneliness beneath the All-seeing Eye,
as they glowed on the day when Hagar wept on
their borders, and God answered the helpless
gushing of a slave-woman's tears, with the
" special Providence" of a miraculous and angel-
guarded fountain!

We believe, or we do *not* believe : *if* we
believe, it must be on the good old-fashioned
Scriptural belief, that "the very hairs of our
" head are numbered"; that Heaven has its own
inscrutable means of working out its own inscrutable designs; that God's ways are not as
our ways; that His Providence guards the low-
est, as it guards the highest; and that whether
from high or low, its instruments are chosen by
a selection of its own!

Mysterious to us are the rules by which it
works: but among the most obvious effects of
those rules upon earth, is this which all history
teaches; viz., that in all cases of great injustice

among men, there comes a culminating point, after which that injustice *is not borne:* whether that point arrive on the wrong of a peasant or the wrong of a king. Things ripen in health and in disease: ripen alike for bloom and for disgust. There is no standing still, in a world which God set moving.

In our little corner of the earth,—where so much besides is busy and fermenting for change, —the time is ripely come for alteration in the laws for women. And they will be changed.

In vain would the sneerers declare, " This is folly ; this is the mere rebellion of a clever woman against the authority of her natural lord and master." It is not so. Real superiority will make itself felt—and my heart bows low and reverentially before it, for I hold that it does not depend on the glitter of human gifts. That man is not my superior who has greater comeliness of appearance, or a quicker human intelligence; but he that is better, stronger-hearted, and a more faithful servant of God. He who stands nearer to glory than I, on that ladder to Heaven which angels tread; and will so stand in its clear light, when human comeliness shall be black mould, and the sparkle of human intelligence—darkness.

Madam,—in families, as in nations, Rebellion
is a disease that springs from the *malaria* of bad
government. WRONGS make REBELS. Those
who would dwell submissive in the wholesome
atmosphere of authority, revolt in the jail fever
of tyranny.

There is tyranny in these laws which uphold
the strong against the weak; which make so
monstrous a difference between rich and poor.
It ought not to be *possible*, in this realm of
England, that poor men should be able to say,—
" We are brought up for judgment before these
" gentlemen, because laws are made against *us*,
" but not against *them: we* get six months'
" prison for ill-treating our wives, but gentle-
" men seem able to do as they please. *We* get
" twelve months (as Lord Brougham has said)
" for the embezzlement or theft of a few pence,
" —but *they* can creep out of a money contract,
" and no law to check them. *We* go to prison
" for bigamy, because we aint rich enough to
" buy a divorce act; but, as for the rich man,
" who *can* pay for a divorce act, his bigamy sets
" his son among the gentry, or among the peers
" of England, and his lady among the other
" ladies of the land. Our hearts revolt against
" being judged by men who are, in fact, more

" guilty than ourselves, though we are prisoners,
" and some of them are magistrates." By a
very recently enacted statute, the law compels
the poor man to be responsible to the community at large, for the maltreatment of his wife.
Why should it seem grievous and shocking to
make new laws of restraint for gentlemen as
well as for poor men? Is the right of ill-usage
a luxury belonging (like the possibility of divorce) to the superior and wealthy classes?

It ought not to be possible either, in this
realm of England, that the spirit of sectarianism
should be stronger than the spirit of justice.
In the Parliamentary Debates of last session,
(March 1, 1854), no less than twelve closely-
printed columns of the "Times" newspaper are
filled with speeches from various members, rela-
tive to an inquiry into the treatment of Roman
Catholic ladies in the conventual establishments
of their religion; and, on another occasion, with
the battling whether a Catholic gentleman should
or should not be able to put his daughters to a
Catholic school; the school-girl's letters being
gravely read to the assembled Senate of England.
What an impulse to humanity is an adverse
creed! Who would believe that these Protestant
debaters, so anxious to control Roman Catholics

in their domestic relations, are utterly revolted at the idea of submitting to any control them-selves! That these careful guardians of female property, who are struck with horror at the idea of a young heiress being "over-persuaded" to give her money to a nunnery,—will placidly see any amount of fraud committed, as long as it is merely in their own Protestant circle. There is more fervour and ferment as to the hanging of garlands in Knightsbridge Church, or the placing of Christ's emblem on Miss Sellon's altar, than in any debate for the amendment of the Marriage Laws, that has been forced on the reluctant attention of Parliament!

Neither ought it to be possible that the pleasures of a few idlers should be better protected than the female portion of a whole community. If Mr Norton, a magistrate and member of the aristocracy, had cheated at a game of cards in one of the clubs of London, all England would have been in a ferment. Nay, even if he had refused to pay a "debt of honour"—to a *man*—it would have been reckoned a most startling and outrageous step! But, because the matter is only between him and his wife,—because it is "only a woman,"—the whole complexion of the case is altered. Only a woman! whom he can

libel with impunity, to find a loophole for escape
or excuse.

I declare, upon the holy sacraments of God,
that I was *not* Lord Melbourne's mistress; and,
what is more, I do not believe (and nothing
shall ever make me believe), that Mr Norton
ever thought that I was. In that miserable fact
is the root of all my bitterness, and of all his
inconsistency! He never had a real conviction
(not even an unjust one), to make him con-
sistent. He wavered, because he was doing,
not what he thought necessary and just, but
what he imagined would "*answer:*" and sometimes one thing appeared likely to answer and
sometimes another. He thought the course he
took respecting me and my children, in 1836,
would answer; and so far it did answer, that he
is two thousand a-year the richer. He thought
his defence to the tradesman's action, in 1853,
would answer; and so far it did answer, that he
is five hundred a-year the richer. But he never
believed the accusations on which he has twice
founded his gainful measures of expediency. He
acknowledged he did not believe them, to others
who have published his acknowledgment.

It ought not to be *possible* that any man, by
mock invocations to justice, should serve a mere

purpose of interest or vengeance; it ought not
to be *possible* that any man should make "the
"law" his minister, in seeking not that which is
just, but that which may "answer."

I appeal whether this ought to be! Beyond
the factious sectarianism which sees no interest
in debates, unless they unfurl the standard of
religious war! Beyond the circle of protected
whist-players; and the few Haynaus of polite
society who see no reason for interference in the
insult and degradation of English women, though
they raise an outcry at the barbarous custom of
other countries! Beyond the senate occupied
with a hot discussion whether dogs shall be permitted to draw carts,—whether the arms of
Scotland are properly quartered with the arms
of England,—whether Roman Catholic gentlemen shall send their children to Roman Catholic
schools,—but not with the laws of protection for
their own wives, sisters, and daughters! I appeal from these sects and sections to the wider
England: to the mercantile classes,—the working lawyers,—the tradespeople (who are cheated
by these laws),—and to the common sense of the
general Parliament of Great Britain. It is not
fit there should be one law for the poor and
another for the rich,—one law for the weak, and

another for the strong,—one law for England,
and another for Scotland: and that the effect of
this confusion should be (by the admission of
law-givers themselves), scandal, outrage, and
fraud; and an impossibility of earrying out the
ends of justice.

There is needed in England, what is established by law in other countries; a tribunal for
marriage and divorce cases, with full power of
control; and why that power cannot be vested
in the Court of Chancery (as the Lord Chancellor proposed), it is for the legists who contradicted him to shew. One argument against it
is probably entirely fallacious; and that is the
enormous increase of business which these family
disputes would bring: (even if we are to admit,
that justice should not be administered if its
administration is to become troublesome.) The
same argument was used when the Infant Custody Bill was passed. Lord Wynford then declared that, in consequence of this bill, " *the*
" *judges would have a burden thrown upon them,*
" *which their other duties rendered them wholly*
" *unable to bear. The husband, besides, would be*
" *kept in a constant state of litigation from one end*
" *of the year to the other.*"

We have now fifteen years' experience to judge

the bill upon. Has that been the result? On the contrary, the exact truth and clearsightedness of the answers made by Lord Lyndhurst, and the then Lord Chancellor, have been proved to demonstration:—"*If the husband were to feel* "*that there was a Power of Control residing* "*somewhere, he would not compel his wife to have* "*recourse to an application for its exercise in her* "*behalf*. . . . *The bill, in fact, took the matter* "*out of the hands of the husband, and placed it in* "*the hands of the independent judges of the highest* "*tribunals in the country. All the bill said, was,* "*that the husband should not be judge in his own* "*case*."

Why should he be judge in his own case, in this, more than in any other litigated matter? Why should there be such a dread of establishing a controlling power over husbands? A good and just man need not fear that power; and why is a bad and unjust man to defy the possibility of its exercise?

Here is Lord Melbourne's opinion in my case: the opinion of that minister whose defence is sufficient for Prince Albert, but not sufficient for *me* :—" *Never, to be sure, was there such con-* "*duct! To set on foot that sort of inquiry with-* "*out the slightest real ground for it! But it does*

" *not surprise me. I have always known that*
" *there was there a mixture of ·folly and violence*
" *which might lead to any absurdity or any injus-*
" *tice. Keep up your spirits; agitate yourself as*
" *little as possible; do not be too anxious about*
" *rumours and the opinion of ' the world;' being,*
" *as you are, innocent and in the right, you will,*
" *in the end, bring everything round.*
   " *Yours*,   MELBOURNE."

Why is any man to have uncontrolled licence
to commence a prosecution " *without the slightest
real ground for it?*" Why is the fact of being
innocent and " in the right " to go for nothing
in English law,—and why is the wife in such a
case to have no more claim on the husband than
if she were divorced?

Instead of my having any respect for these
laws, they must of necessity, to me, appear simply ridiculous. In vain would those who desire
to see them maintained, affect to sneer down my
efforts to expose their absurdity, by affirming
that this is a " private quarrel," which ought to
be kept private. It is not in the private quarrel
they are invited to interfere, but in the state of
the English law. That can hardly be called a
private quarrel, which began in a public prosecu-

tion: but if it be a private wrong, it ought to be redressible by public justice. A private quarrel,—what other quarrel can law adjust? What were laws made for, but for redress of private wrongs? Were they made, to decide disputes among nations? WAR is for nations: LAW is for individuals, and in that country where private wrongs cannot be remedied, national justice is at fault! A very shallow reader of history might prove, that from time immemorial, changes in the laws of nations have been brought about by individual examples of oppression. Such examples *cannot* be unimportant, for they are, and ever will be, the little hinges on which the great doors of justice are made to turn.

That my case may be one such example, is no very ambitious hope. That the laws may be changed in your Majesty's reign,—in the reign of a woman and a Queen,—no very exaggerated dream of romance. My miseries date from the time of your Majesty's accession. The years that you have spent as a happy wife and mother, I have spent in a continual struggle for justice. The minister whose name and whose authority is advanced by your Majesty to justify by acclamation the Prince Consort, is quoted by *my*

husband as a means and a cause for my perpetual injury.

It is impossible for me, when I reflect on my
unjust position as an English subject, not also
to reflect on your Majesty's position, as Queen
of the country where such laws are in force:
and on the peculiar circumstances which,—even
had the case occurred to persons obscure and
unknown, instead of to your Majesty's Prime
Minister,—would warrant the hope, that the
present Sovereign of England might take peculiar interest in the reform of the laws which
have made such events possible.

Not lone and vainglorious, like the virgin
Queen Elizabeth,—nor childless, like the hypo-
chondriac Mary,—nor heirless, like the feeble-
minded Anne,—more of " the beauty of woman-
" hood" adorns the destiny of Queen Victoria,
than has belonged to the barren reigns of former
English Queens; and the link to all the interests
of woman's life should be greater. More mercy
may be expected from her, than from the embit-
tered daughter of wronged Catherine of Spain,—
more love, than from the haughty scion of degrad-
ed Anne Boleyn,—more justice, than from the
weak and capricious niece of Charles II.,—more
thankfulness to God, and willingness to help His

less fortunate creatures, may be supposed to exist in the heart of that royal wife and mother, who has been permitted by Him to sail so far on the sea of life, without one storm (as yet) to ruffle its changeful surface!

In the history of those preceding female reigns, I find no trace of any attempt to better the condition of laws for women.

In the hard, stern, persecuting reign of her whose mother had been set aside for the sake of the " Gospel light" that shone in Boleyn's eyes, —women were burnt for faith's sake; and that gentle and learned " child-wife," Lady Jane Grey, suffered unreprieved, for the ambition of others. Sending her last patient sigh to heaven, on the same day (christened Black Monday), that fifteen gibbets were erected for other executions. Mary was gloomy and pitiless: forsaken, like her mother, by a king sooner wearied (and more justly wearied) than her inconstant father, she left no trace of woman's softness to relieve the fierce and joyless history of her brief rule over England.

Nor Anne; though governed by waiting women and female favourites; though the poor crowned slave of the passionate Duchess of Marlborough, and the wily intrigante Mrs

Masham; though as "womanly" as folly could make her, and the incapacity for a great position; feebly declaring, during the quarrels of Harley and Bolingbroke, that "the disputes of her minis- "ters would kill her." (A disease which, fortunately for us, is less dangerous in the present reign; considering the height to which the fever of such disputes has risen.) In all the thirteen years of her non-government, we find no further protection of women than for the sake of that which is always made the *one* plea of protection in mercantile England—property: and we are rather startled than satisfied, when we read, that under Queen Anne, one Haagen Swensden was tried and executed "for stealing and marrying "Mistress Pleasant Rawlins," because she was an heiress.

In Elizabeth's reign—the Queen who preceded Anne, and immediately followed stern Mary— matters were even worse; as indeed they should be; for those women whose positions ought (one would imagine) to teach them most mercy, are often the most severe. The unjust degradation, —the cruel execution,—the vainly touching appeals,—of her mother, Anne Boleyn, (that mother who is by historians stated to have bowed her heart to her licentious husband in her last

miserable letter, that he might show kindness to
her child), taught Elizabeth no tenderness, and
inspired her with no pardon for those of her
own sex who offended her. We are told to
believe her chaste: to believe that she took
hearts but never gave one: that the barren
pleasure of vanity superseded the contemned
passion of love: that she dazzled and flattered
the young, ardent, and comely, only to wean
them from others, not to secure them for herself:
that she broke the heart of some foolish Amy
Robsart, without viewing the gain of a suitor in
any other light than as a conqueror views the
gain of a province: that she no more knew
the meaning of Göethe's yearning and regretful
lines : —

> „Sein hoher Gang,—Sein' edle Gestalt,
> Seines Mundes Lächeln,—Seiner Augen Gewalt,
> Und seiner Rede Zauberfluß,
> Sein Händedruck,—und ach sein Kuß!"

than we know the meaning of the cabalistic
Abracadabra in old books of magic. Let us
believe it. Let there be " no scandal about
" Queen Elizabeth."

In the reign, then, of this " throned Vestal,"
justice was so corruptly administered, that, in

the tenth and last parliament she held, one of
the members described a magistrate as " *a per-*
" *son who, for a dozen chickens, would dispense*
" *with half a dozen penal statutes.*" Her haughty
and uncurbed temper struck, with the fierceness
of a hawk, at all who had the misfortune to
offend her. When Lady Catherine Grey married
the Earl of Hertford, they were divorced by
the Queen's directions, after they had had two
sons ; and both were imprisoned and fined.
When Norfolk attempted to marry the Queen of
Scots, she sent him to the Tower. When Charles,
Earl of Lenox, married Elizabeth Cavendish,
she imprisoned *the mothers* of the newly-wedded
pair. When Leicester married the Earl of
Essex's widow, she consigned him to prison—
not for his sinful love — but for her queenly
jealousy. When Throgmorton was supposed to
love, and plot the escape of, Mary Queen of
Scots, he was racked three times, and afterwards executed; and she vainly attempted to
force on Mary's choice her own creature Dudley,
in the earlier days, before the axe of the execu-
tioner appeared the readiest way of cutting the
Gordian knot of state difficulties; before the
daughter of Anne Boleyn, whose mother had
perished on the scaffold, signed with her own

hand the warrant that was to send another Queen to the scaffold; and heard the same guns boom in triumph, that sounded rough music in her father's ears,—when they sent their wild echo of freedom from London to Richmond, to tell him her mother was a headless corpse.

And with all these heavy governings of the living destinies and sorrowful deaths of others, see what a true " woman" this great queen was. Read the account of her, in the last two years of her life; after the more healthy and animated energy was over, which caused her to box Lord Essex's ears, and that petted favourite to exclaim, " That he would not have taken such an insult " from her father, much less a king in petticoats." Read the account given by Sir John Harrington (her godson) and others,—which describe her frowning on all her ladies, walking about her privy chamber, stamping at ill news, thrusting her rusty sword into the arras in her great rage; *swearing* much,—" to the no small discomfiture " of those about her, especially our sweet Lady " Arundel;" " or chiding for small neglect, in such " wise as to make these fayre maides often cry and " bewaile in piteous sort;" and finally (fearing to go to bed lest she should never rise again) sitting for ten days on cushions on the ground; generally with her finger in her mouth, and her eyes bent on the earth: till she died, and was buried, (at an expense of £17,428), and her ransacked wardrobe attested her feminine love of finery, by countless sets of jewels, and upwards of two thousand different dresses!

In this reign, the carrying off of an heiress, and rape, were made felony without benefit of clergy; but then that severe protection was also given to those who suffered robbery to the amount of five shillings in a house or out-house; so that the protection of women remained much where it was. In the reign of George I. one of Queen Anne's maids of honour, Mary Forester,—having been married when twelve years old to Sir George Downing, and that ungallant baronet, on returning from his travels, declaring that she was not at all to his taste, that he would have nothing to say to her, and that he utterly declined taking her to wife;—" was persuaded to " prefer a petition to the House of Lords to be " divorced." All the bishops, and a majority of the peers, were against granting this divorce; and Mary Forester remained nominal Lady Downing.

The reign of George III. and of the precise Queen Charlotte, began with a proclamation against vice and profaneness; yet in September, 1771, that is, eleven years after the proclamation, there were twenty-five cases pending in Doctor's Commons, being a greater number than for fifty years before: and in the summer preceding, a subject recovered £10,000 damages against one of the royal dukes (damages having been laid at £100,000). Even then, the law seem to have followed its usual rule of confusion in support of morality; for in the same year it occurred that two persons received an equal punishment of being whipped round Covent Garden; one of those persons having seduced his own niece, while the other—*had stolen a bunch of radishes.*

That, however, was a degree better than the proportion of the present day; when (as Lord Brougham has shown) some defect in the working of " Justice's justice," may consign a poor man to prison for twelve months for stealing to the value of threepence; and a gentleman may do pretty nearly as he pleases. It is a state of things that will not be borne much longer; we are anxious that the people should learn a modern version of the lesson taught a century ago in " Ward's Rhyming Dialogues " about the study of " Common Things." They will turn their attention also to the study of " Uncommon Things;" and amongst the most remarkable of common, or uncommon, subjects for reflection, are the inequalities of justice. A thing will be borne at one time, that will become an impossibility at another. In the summer of 1717, two soldiers were whipped almost to death, and turned out of the service, only for wearing oakboughs in their hats on the 29th of May. What would have been said or done under such circumstances the 29th of last May? About six years before, when Sir Cholmondely Dering was killed in a duel, an attempt was made to bring in a bill against duelling, which it was found utterly impossible to pass; but, in 1765, Lord Byron stood his trial before the Peers for killing Mr Chaworth; in 1804, a jury convicted Captain Best of wilful murder for his fatal duel with Lord Camelford; and, in 1808, Major Campbell was executed for his fatal duel with Captain Boyd. Who thinks of fighting a duel now? Or, who thinks of a hundred other changes, as complete and more important?

And now it is the fashion amongst legists to work very heartily at " *assimilating* " this law and that law,—" assimilating " the law of evidence in England and Scotland; and the law of partnership; and the commercial law for bills of exchange. On this last, the Lord Advocate observes, that "*it is a matter of astonishment that* "*the law of bills of exchange has remained so long* "*in the barbarous state it is at present.*" And Sir Erskine Perry (who has been in India) says, much remains to do, but much has been done since Bentham's time, when the field of English law was "a wild jungle." Does it not occur to these and other authorities, that the law of "*might is right*" savours also rather of the "wild jungle," than of the calm enactments of a civilised Christian country? and that the principle of "assimilation" might be extended with advantage to those laws between husband and wife, which are utterly at variance North and South of the river Tweed?

Twenty years ago, the Warrender case occupied public attention; and Lord Brougham, when speaking on that case, summed up, in his usual graphic manner, the absurd contradictions involved by the conflict of Scotch and English law. Lord Lyndhurst, following in the same case, and remarking on the same absurdities, stated that Lord Eldon had intended to bring in a Bill to reconcile the difference between the laws of the two countries. Where is the Bill of

that sagacious old lawyer, whose countenance so
much resembled the physiognomy of the bird of
Minerva, that Sydney Smith said, " no man ever
could *be* as wise, as Lord Eldon *looked?* " At
the end of twenty years from that declaration of
Lord Lyndhurst's, we are still pottering over
piecemeal changes: still bringing in feeble Bills
to " prevent Border marriages," or fine those
who " witness" weddings at Gretna Green!
Actually, many of our own legislators, and all
the foreigners I ever talked with on the subject,
believe Gretna to be an exceptional town, or
spot, where marriage is possible by some exceptional law; not knowing that Gretna is merely
the nearest place for English parties to avail
themselves of Scotch law,—the nearest point in
Scotland English lovers can reach. Irish parties
did not go to Gretna. Irish parties eloped to
Port Patrick, and were married there, as the
nearest point in Scotland *they* could reach; and
it may perhaps amaze my readers to learn, that
the Scotch complained of English immorality,
and attributed their skipping across their borders,
to an attempt to make marriages they could
afterwards evade by English law; cheating the
innocent Caledonians into unions with them,
and afterwards discarding the objects of their

choice; and the Scotch themselves, consequently endeavoured to prevent these Border marriages. Yet here we are, still labouring over this knotty point: these Cyclops of the law, who can only see with one eye, narrowly peeping at, and puzzling over, one single aspect of their many difficulties; when it must be obvious to common sense, on a broad general view of those difficulties, that what is needed is an " assimilation " of the law,—what is needed is, that the Northern portion and Southern portion of your Majesty's dominions should be brought under *one* law; and there the conflict would cease.

There the conflict would cease. I do not say, there a better protection would begin; for I cannot prophesy whether Lord Cranworth's views, or those of Lords Eldon, Thurlow, and Rosslyn, would preponderate ; whether, in the "assimilation" that would take place, a better mercy to women would be borrowed from portions of the Scotch law, or the Desdemonas of Scotland be smothered by a jealous English legislation.

But this I will venture to say: that in no country in Europe is there *in fact* so little protection of women, as in England! In France a married woman may be arrested for debt; but

in France a married woman is under the careful
protection of the law, and her husband under the
strict control of the law; indeed, the law of
France views the position of women with peculiar indulgence. In Germany, Austria, Prussia,
Holland, Sweden, and Russia, (as I will prove by
a handbook of those laws which I am preparing
for the press,) the rules of interference for the
protection of married women are infinitely more
favorable than in our own country.

I have, as I said before, learned the English
law piecemeal, by suffering under it. My husband is a lawyer; and he has taught it me, by
exercising over my tormented and restless life,
every quirk and quibble of its tyranny; of its
acknowledged tyranny;—acknowledged, again I
say, not by wailing, angry, despairing women,
but by Chancellors, ex-Chancellors, legal reformers, and members of both Houses of Parliament. And yet nothing is done! indeed,
when the Solicitor-General, May 10th, in this
session, informed the House that the delayed
Marriage Bill would be brought forward "as
"soon as the House had expressed an opinion on
"the Testamentary Jurisdiction Bill," there was
a good-humoured laugh at the very vague pros-
pect held out,—but nobody murmured ; for

nobody greatly cared when it should come on; or whether it ever came on at all.

Nevertheless, so long as human nature is what it is, some marriages must be unhappy marriages, instead of following that theory of intimate and sacred union which they ought to fulfil: and the question is, therefore, what is to be the relation of persons living in a state of alienation, instead of a state of union,—all the existing rules for their social position being based on the first alternative,—namely, that they *are* in a state of union,—and on the supposition that marriage is indissoluble, though Parliament has now decided that it is a civil contract? Divorced or undivorced, it is absolutely necessary that the law should step in, to arrrange that which is disarranged by this most unnatural condition. It becomes perfectly absurd that the law which appoints the husband legal protector of the woman, should not (failing him who has ceased to be a protector, and has become a very powerful foe) itself undertake her protection. She stands towards the law, by an illustration which I have repeatedly made use of,—in the light of an ill-used inferior; and she is the *only* inferior in England who cannot claim to be so protected.

Those women who desire to learn, in a more

formal and direct manner, what the laws are,—
have only to refer to Macqueen, Ferguson,
Hosack, and other law writers. There they
may read,—that if a collection could be made of
all municipal rules as to divorce, it "would
appear little better than a ludicrous exhibition of
human inconsistency and caprice;" that, till the
celebrated Council of Trent, even the Roman
Catholic Church had been "constantly shifting to
all points between the opposite extremes on the
subject of divorce ;" that under the Greek
Church, and in the Protestant states of Europe,
the utmost diversity of rules still prevails,—
"from the extreme of refusing to give divorce
" *a vinculo*, even for adultery,—to the opposite ex-
"treme of allowing dissolution of marriage for
"causes which our law accounts perfectly frivo-
"lous;" that when the Council of Trent promul-
gated its canons *De sacramento Matrimonii*, the
same chapter which said, "Accursed is he who
"affirms that marriage can be made dissoluble,"
also contained a similar anathema against any
one who should affirm marriage to be a superior
condition to virginity or a state of celibacy—
any one who should affirm it superstitious to
forbid marriage at certain seasons of the year—
or any one *who denied that the right of jurisdiction*

*in matrimonial cases belongs to the Ecclesiastical
Courts;* under which last canon will come Lords
Cranworth and Campbell, and all the Peers and
Commons voting with them for reform in the
piecemeal law of England;—of that country
which publishes a Liturgy for its Established
Church, containing a Roman Catholic ceremony
for marriage; overrules the vows of that ceremony by Acts of Parliament; evades them by
the Marriage Registration Act; solemnly quotes
them, as an argument for keeping women to the
indissoluble bond; and sets them at defiance (as a
form involving no legal obligation), when the
indissoluble bond is to be broken for men!

There, also, women may comfort themselves
by reading, that Lord Eldon, after thirty years'
experience in the highest court of judicature in
the kingdom, reversed his earlier opinions, and
stated that he " saw no reason why a woman
" was not as much entitled to sue for divorce as
" a man:"—that Mr Hallam writes,—" Nothing
" can be more absurd than our modern *privile-*
" *gia;* our Acts of Parliament to break the
" marriage bond; neither do I see how we can
" justify the denial of redress to women, in every
" case of adultery and desertion:"—that Mon-
tesquieu affirmed the law to be " very tyran·

" nical" which gives the right to men and denies it to women;—adding, that women are less likely to abuse the privilege than men, because a woman rarely improves her position by repudiating her husband.

They may read Milton, Gibbon, and Hume, —or the more pious Paley,—in such chapters and sections of these authors as treat on the subject. They may read also, how the Scotch and English subjects of Queen Victoria are as differently dealt with as though they were subjects of two different countries, and under two different sovereigns ; and how, from time to time, great and clever men have expressed their opinion of the absolute necessity of " assimilat-" ing " those conflicting laws.

They may read lists of the names of those at present employed in law offices under the crown : and find, to their amazement,—in that helpless group who consider these reforms " so sur-" rounded with difficulty," that they can do nothing,—Lord Chancellor Cranworth, and Lord Chief Justice Campbell, heading famous and familiar lawyer-names; some, with already an hereditary claim to distinction, and some, whose able and energetic pleading will make their names a boast to their sons. They may refer

to the former speeches of men like Lyndhurst
and Brougham,—whose celebrity began so early
in life, that they are still here to enjoy and add
to it; though their youthful triumphs are almost a matter of history to the rising genera-
tion. All this, women may study: and when
they have read all which they have time, pa-
tience, or inclination to read, and ability to
understand,—they may take their crochet-work,
embroidery, or " Potichomanie," and ruminate
over their needles and paste-brushes, how it is
that laws continue to be in force, which such
men themselves have so repeatedly condemned,
as a mass of folly, indecency, and contradiction!

I hope, during this period of tranquil reflection, the rebellious thought may not occur to
the tapestry-working sex, that the obstacle to
this legal reform must be, that men fear to curb
the license of their own pleasures. It is impossible, seeing how eager, energetic, and enthu-
siastic, men are in *other* reforms whose necessity
is once proved and admitted, not to fancy that
the reason why this particular change is " *so*
" *surrounded with difficulty*" is because it is extremely unpalatable to the reformers! I think
—to use the words of the Solicitor-General—

the House " will express an opinion on the Tes-
" tamentary Jurisdiction Bill" with infinitely
more speed, clearness, and decision, than on a
Marriage Reform Bill. Every man seems to
dread that he is surrendering some portion of
his own rights over woman, in allowing these
laws to be revised; even while he admits that
abuses which are " a disgrace to England," blot
the strange barbarous code, which remains intact
while other barbarous laws have gradually been
repealed or altered.

To all that women can read on the subject, I
add this more familiarly easy treatise; and I
shall follow this treatise by a published selection
of " *Cases, decided according to Law, and con-
" trary to Justice;*" admitted to be so decided even
by the judges and counsel engaged in them;
the sentences given being often accompanied by
courteous and sincere expressions of regret at
their manifest oppression; and by a hope that
the code might be altered, which made such sentences compulsory on the persons whose duty it
was "to administer the law as they found it."
My husband has taught me, by subpœnaing my
publishers to account for my earnings,– that my
gift of writing was not meant for the purposes to
which I have hitherto applied it. It was not

intended that I should "strive for peace and "ensue it" through a life of much occasional bitterness and many unjust trials; that I should prove my literary ability, by publishing melodies and songs for young girls and women to sing in happier homes than mine,—or poetry and prose for them to read in leisure hours,—or even please myself by better and more serious attempts to advocate the rights of the people, or the education and interests of the poor.

When Mr Norton allowed me, I say, to be publicly subpœnaed in court, to defend himself by a quibble from a just debt, and subpœnaed my publishers to meet me there, he taught me what my gift of writing was worth. Since he would not leave even *that* source tranquil and free in my destiny, let him have the triumph of being able at once to embitter and to turn its former current. He has made me dream that it was meant for a higher and stronger purpose, —that gift which came not from man, but from God. It was meant to enable me to rouse the hearts of others to examine into all the gross injustice of these laws,—to ask the "nation of "gallant gentlemen," whose countrywoman I am, for once to hear a woman's pleading on the subject. Not because I deserve more at their hands

than other women. Well I know, on the con·
trary, how many hundreds, infinitely better than
I,—more pious, more patient, and less rash
under injury,—have watered their bread with
tears! My plea to attention is, that in pleading
for myself I am able to plead for all these
others. Not that my sufferings or my deserts
are greater than theirs; but that I combine,
with the fact of having suffered wrong, the
power to comment on and explain the cause of
that wrong; which few women are able to do.

For *this*, I believe, God gave me the power of
writing. To this I devote that power. I abjure
all other writing, till I see these laws altered.
I care not what ridicule or abuse may be the
result of that declaration. They who cannot
bear ridicule and abuse, are unfit and unable to
advance *any* cause: and once more I deny that
this is my personal cause; it is the cause of all
the women of England. If *I* could be justified and
happy to-morrow, I would still strive and labour
in it; and if I were to die to-morrow, it would
still be a satisfaction to me that I had so striven.
Meanwhile, my husband has a legal lien (as he
has publicly proved), on the copyright of my
works. Let him claim the copyright of THIS:

M

and let the Lord Chancellor, whose office is
thus described in Chamberlayne's State of England,"—" *To judge, not according to the Common*
" *Law, as other Civil Courts do, but to moderate*
" *the rigour of the Law, and to judge according to*
" *Equity, Conscience, and Reason: and his Oath*
" *is to do right to all manner of People, poor and*
" *rich, after the Laws and Customs of the Realm,*
" *and truly counsel the King,*"—let the Lord
Chancellor, I say,—the " Summus Cancellarius"
of Great Britain, cancel, in Mr Norton's favour,
—according to the laws and customs of this
realm of England,—my right to the labour of
my own brain and pen; and docket it, among
forgotten Chancery Papers, with a parody of
Swift's contemptuous labelling.

" *Only a Woman's Pamphlet.*"

But let the recollection of what I write, remain with those who read; and above all, let
the recollection remain with your Majesty, to
whom it is addressed; the one woman in England who *cannot* suffer wrong; and whose royal
assent will be formally necessary to any Marriage Reform Bill which the Lord Chancellor,
assembled Peers, and assembled Commons, may

think fit to pass, in the Parliament of this
free nation; where, with a Queen on the throne,
all other married women are legally "NON-EX-
ISTENT."

I remain,

With the sincerest loyalty and respect,

Your Majesty's humble and devoted

Subject and Servant,

CAROLINE ELIZABETH SARAH NORTON.

No. 3, CHESTERFIELD STREET, MAY FAIR,
This 2nd day of June, 1855.

For EU product safety concerns, contact us at Calle de José Abascal, 56–1°,
28003 Madrid, Spain or eugpsr@cambridge.org.

www.ingramcontent.com/pod-product-compliance
Ingram Content Group UK Ltd.
Pitfield, Milton Keynes, MK11 3LW, UK
UKHW012340130625
459647UK00009B/417